Adriana,

I hope you enjoy my letters!

All the Best,
Dan

Letters to my
"AMERICAN"
Babies

A Gringo Dad's Thoughts on Life, Liberty and the True Meaning of Happiness

Danny Gardner

First published in the United States by Danny Gardner

Copyright © Danny Gardner, 2019
All rights reserved

THE LIBRARY OF CONGRESS HAS CATALOGUED THE PAPERBACK VERSION OF THIS BOOK AS FOLLOWS:

Gardner, Danny
Letters to My "American" Babies-A Gringo Dad's Thoughts on Life, Liberty and the True Meaning of Happiness

ISBN: 978-0-578-43737-8

Printed in the United States of America

To my beautiful American Babies,
Nicolas, Isabella and Valentina

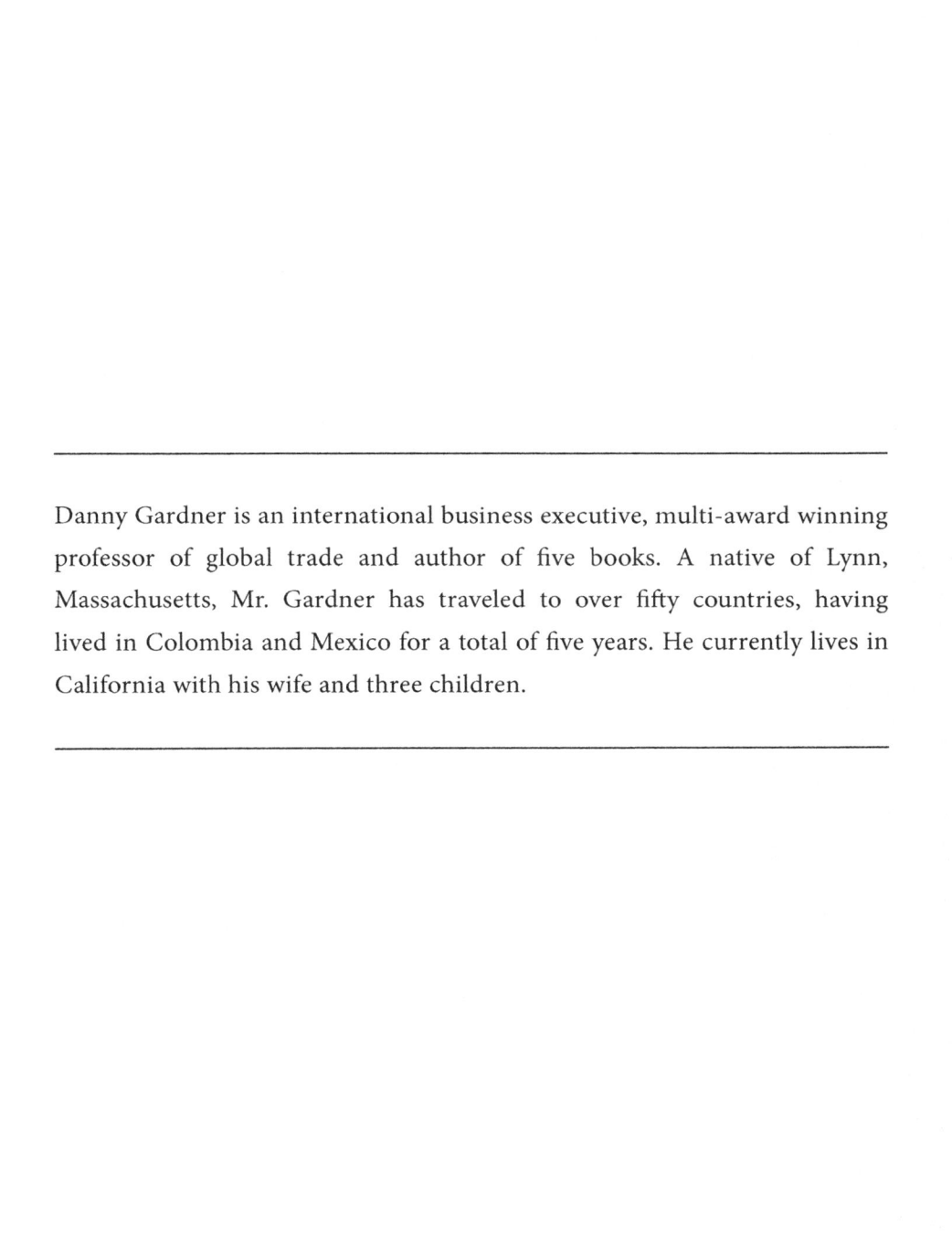

Danny Gardner is an international business executive, multi-award winning professor of global trade and author of five books. A native of Lynn, Massachusetts, Mr. Gardner has traveled to over fifty countries, having lived in Colombia and Mexico for a total of five years. He currently lives in California with his wife and three children.

ME SALE DEL CORAZÓN

A mis adorados nietos Nicolás, Isabella y Valentina,

He leído y releído las cartas de Daniel a sus "American Babies," siempre luchando entre la emoción y las lágrimas para entender la historia de una vida creada, cuidada y amada por dos seres con culturas diferentes. Dos vidas que se han mezclado en la felicidad y el amor para constituir una familia que se integra sin límites culturales, pero con un eslabón que las une…el respeto.

Esta misma colección de cartas se ha construido desde la historia y testimonios de vida, de unos ancestros familiares que se remontan al pasado para llegar como una melodía a las realidades de la vida de hoy.

Como historia, cada carta tiene una ubicación del entorno que vivía la sociedad americana en su momento. Cada vivencia explica la reciedumbre y los valores de sus actores…los miembros de la Familia Gardner-Serna y sus progenitores, cada uno con orígenes culturales bien diferentes.

Cuando empecé a leer "Letters To My American Babies" entré en confusión porque no podía entender si era la historia de una familia que se construía sobre los ancestros y la cultura, o si era un medio de comunicación entre el padre y sus hijos, en el cuál Daniel escogió el método epistolar para dejar lecciones de vida a sus babies.

Al sentirme parte de la historia, mi corazón no paraba de latir, porque también recordé momentos de vida de mis ancestros y los valores que nos inculcaban. Estos son los mismos valores que fueron heredados por nuestros hijos y que todavía soportan nuestra unidad familiar. Al final entendí.

Cada carta resume un ciclo de vida con hechos, mensajes y lecciones, pero no solo para recordar el pasado. Al fin y al cabo, son lecciones para "My Babies" de como vivir y construir un futuro, soportado en un pasado que no conocieron, ni vivieron, pero que serán los cimientos para construir su propia vida y las de sus familias. Todo esto tendrá que pasar en un mundo bien diferente al pasado, con retos y desafíos por descubrir.

Esta es una obra que describe los momentos históricos y los valores de dos culturas que se mezclan en el amor y el respeto para constituir una familia que aprende a vivir, crecer y consolidarse. Este relato ha pasado y seguirá pasando en un ambiente de culturas, prácticas y creencias diversas, con hijos respetuosos y orgullosos de quienes son, y al final, una familia dueña de su propio ADN, lista para que "Los Babies" construyan su propia ruta sin renunciar al pasado, pero listos para enfrentar el futuro.

Los adoro a todos,

El Abuelito Humberto

TABLE OF CONTENTS

LETTER I: The First Letter To My, "American" Babies 1

LETTER II: We're All Americans 5

LETTER III: Define Happiness On Your Own Terms 9

LETTER IV: What Price Freedom? 14

LETTER V: The Dumb End Of The Tape 19

LETTER VI: A Hard Fought "B" Is Better Than An Easy "A" 25

LETTER VII: Love Affair With A Language 30

LETTER VIII: A Tale Of Two Cold Calls 37

LETTER IX: Learning From Our Mistakes (Or Not) 41

PHOTOS 47

LETTER X: 9/11 59

LETTER XI: Schooled 66

LETTER XII: Teddy 70

LETTER XIII: As The Fourth Quarter Begins And Overtime Looms 73

LETTER XIV: Los Abuelitos 76

LETTER XV: Grampa Dick 81

LETTER XVI: Nana Mary 89

LETTER XVII: The Seeker 97

LETTER I

THE FIRST LETTER TO MY "AMERICAN" BABIES

Dear Nicolas, Isabella and Valentina,

When I was a kid, I remember hearing about the year 2000 and how that New Year's celebration would not only end the 20th century, but be the beginning of a new millennium. That all sounded cool, but for a late-seventies teenager growing up on Boston's North Shore, it just seemed too far off to worry about. Eventually, my attitude changed and to this day, January 1, 2000 has a very special meaning for me.

For whatever reason, by the time I graduated high school in 1980 I found myself imagining what my life would look like at the turn of the century. It wasn't an obsession, but I do recall wondering what I'd be doing when 1999 came to an end. I even calculated that I'd be thirty eight on 1/1/2000, an age that was actually wrong (I was born 2/19/62, which put me seven weeks shy of thirty eight…Nice math, dad).

Through a series of events that we'll get into later, New Year's Day 2000 found me standing in front of the new house mom and I had recently bought in Aventura Lakes, Florida. In a scene I never considered, at my side was our first child, Mr. Nicolas Gardner. All of eighteen months old, Nico and I were holding hands and staring off into the South Florida sky when my Big Millennium Question was finally answered.

For all of my dreams of the future, never once did it occur to me that I'd have anyone to worry about other than myself. Every scenario I ever conjured up was all about me…What places will I have visited? Where will I be living? The touch of Nico's hand made me realize that although my journey had been a successful one, my life now had to be about him, and in the years to follow, equally about Bella and Vali.

Fast forward to 2017 and much has changed. We left Florida after 9/11 and spent almost four years living in Guadalajara. From there, we came to Los Angeles in 2005 and the speed with which the last dozen years blew by has left me dumbfounded.

Nico, you have become a splendid young man on the eve of your own Grand Adventure. Bella, at sixteen you are quickly turning into an independent and strong Latina woman with unlimited potential. And Vali, "The Baby," you are the sweetest and most kind twelve year old that a dad could ask for. Great things surely await you.

While the passage of time brings change, there is one thing about our relationship that will always stay the same. Without ever wavering, mom and I will do everything we can to provide you with the guidance, encouragement and love you need to navigate today's so-very-troubled world.

As I've told you many times, our Job Description as parents is a one-liner: "Leave the next generation poised for greater things." Mom and I were both lucky enough to have parents that positioned us for greater things, and you can be sure that we will carry on that tradition.

When I turned fifty in 2012, a golfer friend told me that in terms of remaining birthdays, I was "Playing the back nine." Although I got a good laugh from that joke, it made me think about how sneaky Father Time really is, and that if I was going to live up to my "Greater Things" pledge, there was much work yet to be done.

In the end, life comes down to time and what we choose to do with it. With whatever time I have left, I remain committed to work with mom to give each of you every opportunity to create the lives you seek. But like many parents, I can't help but worry about what your worlds will look like when you become adults and have to make decisions on your own.

So, in addition to whatever advice I've been able to provide you as children, I'm going to start writing you letters that when taken as a whole, may one day serve to guide you as grownups. Overall, I hope to achieve three goals through these letters.

First, I want to share my thoughts on life's "Big Themes." In today's world, it's easy to lose sight of basic stuff like who you want to be as a person, how you will achieve the goals you set and most importantly, what your own unique definition of happiness will be. I'm no expert on the Human Condition, but I do hope that a window into the experiences I've had will serve to take you down a smoother path.

Second, I want to make sure that you know who you are and where you came from. While polar opposites, both sides of our family have an amazing American Story to tell and it is important to understand our history. Each of you is a child of The Age of Globalization and you must go forward in this life equally proud of your Bostonian and Colombian heritages.

Third, and perhaps selfishly, I want to tell you more about myself. Although I had a great relationship with my own dad, I wish I knew more about your Grampa Dick as a person. Growing up as the oldest of six kids in the Great Depression, he was from a generation that kept their feelings to themselves and just toughed things out.

Whereas I have tried over the years to be more open with you, there's lots that I haven't revealed. The topics and tales found in future letters are meant to fill in any blanks there may be between us and to one day spare you from the hauntings of mysteries unsolved.

It is likely that my letters will generate as many questions as they do answers. As a father trying to pass on some hard-earned wisdom to his children, I certainly hope so. In that very spirit, may your first lesson be that questions are a reflection of human curiosity and it will be that same curiosity that keeps your lives interesting and full of purpose.

As you pass from childhood to adulthood, try your best to remain curious, set audacious goals and most of all, soldier on when trouble comes your way.

Do these things and I can guarantee you that you'll emerge a better person for having braved the endeavor.

Over the course of the coming years, it will be through a series letters that I hope to convey the above messages. As time goes by, may you revisit them and take each one as a reminder of how much I love the three of you. If you find value in these letters, may you build on them through your own experiences and leave the next generation of Gardner's poised for even greater things.

With much love,
Fafa

LETTER II

WE'RE ALL AMERICANS

Dear Nico, Bella and Valentina,

I know you guys have heard my, "We're all Americans" rant way too many times, but I never told you the backstory that goes with it. I want to give you the complete version because it's not only a cool window into my days as a globetrotter, it captures the essence of your roots as bi-racial children.

Long before I started travelling the world, I was one of those guys that thought the U.S. was the greatest country ever. Being from Massachusetts and growing up ten miles from places like Paul Revere's House and Bunker Hill, I had a real sense of history, and totally bought into the idea of what is now called, "American Exceptionalism."

When I moved to Colombia for the second time in 1992, I carried that pride of being American with me. That is, until I met a young guy from Argentina on a flight from Manaus to Miami who interrupted a conversation I was having with some work colleagues. I remember it was 2002 because the World Cup was going on and the Argentine spoke up because I was rambling on about the U.S. soccer team.

To begin with, you have to understand that Argentina is a very proud nation and its people also believe that their country is the most important on earth. That belief is especially strong when it comes to "fútbol," so when I started talking nonsense about how good the U.S. soccer team was, it didn't take long for this young fellow to chime in.

After the Argentinean guy let me know that the U.S. team actually stunk and that we didn't have a prayer of winning, I took things up a notch and began spouting out the usual clichés like, "America's the greatest," and "The U.S.A. is number one." And that was when my new friend embarrassed me with a simple truth and taught me a lesson that has stayed with me to this day.

As I said, I was with some work mates and it just so happened that the Argentine was sitting across the aisle from us. I should have known better than to mess with this guy because even though he was younger than me, he was worldlier than I ever dreamed of being. He was a handsome guy, too… blonde hair, blue eyes and to make matters worse, his girlfriend was with him, and she was stunning.

When I was done making a fool of myself, he leaned sideways and said in perfect English, "Hey guy, take a look at a map. In the Western Hemisphere, we're all Americans." The look on my face must have revealed my ignorance, because he glanced at his girl and then back at me in the condescending way that only an Argentinean can do, adding, "Yeah, you know, North Americans and South Americans." And just for added effect, he reiterated his point in Spanish, "Somos todos Americanos, ves?"

I thought about that guy long after I got back to Miami because he was right. Even though we here in the U.S. think we have the franchise on greatness, every person from North or South America certainly has the right to call themselves, "Americans." Actually, I'm confident that the guy for whom The Americas were named, Amerigo Vespucci, would endorse that belief wholeheartedly.

So, that's where the "We're all Americans" line comes from and a lesson that started out as an embarrassment for me, eventually became a source of pride. Think about this for a second…You guys have more of a right to say you're "American" than most anyone born in the U.S.A. because I'm from North America and your mom is from South America.

As an added bonus, my dad's father was actually born in Newfoundland, Canada, so that lends even more credibility to our hemispheric bloodlines. In today's divided and often-times prejudiced world, I think that's a pretty cool claim to be able to make. As a dad, there are few things that bring me greater joy than knowing that my kids are, "Americanos" in every sense of the word.

This story is important because it's kids like you that represent the new look of the United States of America…..bi-racial, multi-cultural and a product of the, "Age of Globalization." Remember, it was the globalization of trade that led me to Colombia, and had it not been for the opening of borders to international business, I never would have met mom and none of you three would even be here.

Because you really are "Americans," you have a number of responsibilities; first to yourselves, but also to your heritage and ultimately, to society in general. Here are some thoughts on what those responsibilities are and why they matter:

First, never turn your back on who you are or where you came from. Don't just be proud of your bi-racial roots, embrace them. After all, there aren't many kids that can say that their dad is Boston (shanty) Irish and that their mom is a full-blooded Colombian beauty. Take the best of both cultures, make them a part of your essential self and go forward in this life as proud Latin Americans.

Second, DO NOT give up on your study of Spanish. Being bilingual is not only a reflection of your ethnicity, having a second language will make you more competitive out in the adult world. If you don't believe that, look at my own experiences…If I hadn't learned Spanish, I never would have been hired to work in Colombia and my life would have been decidedly different (and not for the better).

Of all of my life choices, I can tell you without hesitation that sticking with Spanish was the smartest and most impactful decision I ever made, bar none. Because you guys have been around Spanish since birth and you've lived and travelled in Latin America, you have a huge advantage…Don't blow it through indifference or laziness.

Third, your bi-racial roots should make you more accepting of other people that are "different" from the typical White Bread American (of which, I am admittedly one). Having travelled millions of miles to dozens of countries, I can tell you that there is no superior race, there is no one true religion and there is no single way for people to live their lives.

Fourth, use your experiences as Latinos to build empathy for others minorities. You have a hand-up on society because you look white (OK, maybe not Bella).

That means that you have a bird's eye view into how White America really thinks, especially when you're around people who don't know you're Latinos. You yourselves have been exposed to mild racism, just imagine how not-so-white people must feel.

If there's one last piece of advice that I can give you, it's beware of the word, "Tolerant." In today's politically correct world, we're all taught to be tolerant of one another. Personally, I not only find that word to be ridiculous in the context of race, religion or lifestyle, I actually find it offensive.

Go look up the verb, "to tolerate" in the dictionary and it means to put up with something or somebody that you don't like. Is that really the standard of behavior we're looking for as a society? Is that the bar we've set for our young people? To just put up with one another and avoid any real type of contact with folks that view life differently than us? That's not only boring, it's plain ignorant.

After having travelled hundreds of times to nearly fifty countries and having been exposed to a lot of different situations, one thing I can say for certain is that I avoid "tolerating" people, and I definitely focus more on ACCEPTANCE. Acceptance doesn't necessarily mean that I agree with or even like someone, it just means that I accept their fundamental right to choose a certain way to live.

Actually, I find people that are different from me to be fascinating and a source of not only learning, but also of friendship. I respect the lifestyle choices that people make…I don't "tolerate" the LGBT community or religious groups, I encourage people to do what makes them happy. And that means everybody, whether they're straight, gay, Muslim, gringo, Latino, Asian or anything else, for that matter.

In the end, you should not only pursue the lifestyle that makes you the most happy, you should respect, accept and empathize with people that are different from you. Do these things and trust me when I tell you, you'll be a better (and happier) American for the effort.

Love,
Fafa

LETTER III

DEFINE HAPPINESS ON YOUR OWN TERMS

Dear Nico, Bella and Vali,

As you'll see in all of the letters I write to you, my goal is to share some thoughts on life's Big Themes. There will be many topics we will have touched upon over the months and years, but there's none more important than the idea of, "Defining happiness on your own terms."

According to the ancient Greeks, achieving true happiness should be the driving force in anyone's life. Thomas Jefferson adopted that belief, making it the most quoted line from the Declaration of Independence…every person's right to, "Life, liberty and the pursuit of happiness." While happiness is certainly a right, most people will agree that getting it right is a bit trickier.

Experience has taught me that the first step in achieving long-term happiness is to decide what's important to you. I've said it to you guys a million times, "Life is about priorities and the decisions we make," and one of the most vital decisions that you'll ever face is figuring out what is most important to you. Only then will you be really able to engage in the noble pursuit of happiness.

Whereas your priorities may change over time, deciding what's important boils down to identifying your most basic beliefs. When you can state what it is you believe in, you will then be able to develop the values that guide you. Ideally, it is those beliefs and values that are expressed in your daily behavior by the things that you do. A couple of examples might help to illustrate what I'm trying to say.

Based on some great experiences I had at Salem State College, I came to believe very deeply in the transformational power of education. Specifically, it was the summer of 1981 when I was taking some extra classes before transferring out to American International College. For reasons I'll discuss in another letter, I decided at the age of nineteen that education would be one of my life's Big Themes.

Because I had a fundamental belief in how education could change my life, I placed a lot of value on it. And because education became a core value for me, much of my time, energy and behavior has been channeled in that direction. As both a student and a professor, the never-ending process of learning and self-improvement has brought me great joy over the years.

Another example of deciding what was important to me is my belief in family. As I've told you on many occasions, I had a great relationship with both of my parents and I believed that it was important to invest time and effort in those relationships. Because of that belief, I valued the limited amount of time I had with Grampa Dick and Nana Mary, so I behaved in a way that maximized our time together.

Truth be told, although I knew that my dream of working in Latin American was at greater risk the longer I stayed in Lynn, I remained until age thirty because I wanted to be with my parents, brother and sister. Even after leaving Lynn in 1992, we always made time to meet up in places like Florida and California. Now that both my parents and Uncle Dicky are gone, I'm so glad I made those relationships a priority.

Just so you know, one of the things I love and respect the most about your mother is her own commitment to family. It's easy to see much of what's good about mom by observing the relationship she has with your "Abuelitos," Humberto and Nora. Learn from that relationship, believe in the power of family and invest time not only in your relationships with mom and me, but with each other.

If you buy into the idea that happiness is found by linking beliefs and values to your actions, then it's essential that you continuously look inside yourselves for the roots of those beliefs and values. Only then will you be able to not only decide what your priorities are in life, but also channel those priorities towards your own happiness.

As children, most of your beliefs come from me and mom. From day one, we've instilled in each of you specific values and principles, but for me, I've especially focused on, "Broadening your frame of reference." If you don't recall my many explanations of this term, it's just exposing you to as many experiences as possible so you have a wide perspective on which to build your beliefs.

That's why I've always supported you guys going to Colombia every summer, because I want you to get in touch with your Latino origins, spend time with your Colombian family and see how other cultures live. While mom and I never forced you guys into any activity, it's also why we encourage you to try new things, take risks and have no fear of failure.

When a child starts school, that's when your beliefs and values start to be influenced by friends and classmates. Because California is so diverse and has so many different people, the beliefs and values you were taught at home have often times come in conflict with those of your peers. And that's just fine, as long as you evaluate different viewpoints fairly and use them to build a more evolved Belief System.

Outside of your friend groups, you'll also be influenced by what you see on TV, and especially what you find on Social Media. To be honest, these are the influences that I really worry about because most humans (and especially kids) take their behavioral cues from their leaders and so-called, "Role Models." Trust me when I tell you that much of what you'll find on Social Media is a lesson in how not to behave.

As the father of two teenage girls, you know my thoughts on the Kardashian's and the message they send to young women. For the record, it's not OK to launch a career off of a skanky sex tape and then build, "followers" through endless posts of Botox lips and fake boobs. And it's definitely not OK to make money by making a fool of yourself on TV every night. They're nothing but chusma, money and all.

If you need more lessons in shallow values, look no further than Washington, D.C. Our elected officials and so-called leaders traded their souls for votes a long time ago and in spite of what you see and hear every night on Fox News and CNN, integrity still matters. Lying, stealing and making stuff up is no way to go through life, and the end result of all those nefarious activities will never make you happy.

Ultimately, it will be your own inner voice that makes the final call about what your beliefs, values and behaviors will be. Over time you'll have doubts and wonder if you're on the right path. During those moments of doubt just remember that, "Life is about choices, so listen to the right voices." You should always take advice from people whose opinion you value, but the final voice must always be your own.

What I'm writing about here is similar to what the preacher Rick Warren calls a, "Purpose-Driven Life." I don't have a lot of use for the God Squad, but Rick is right when he says that happiness comes from having a purpose. I can elaborate by saying that a purpose-driven life should be built upon principles-based actions. In other words, being men and women whose actions are guided by our convictions.

I believe that living by your principles can lead to happiness in two ways. First, you can use the beliefs, values and principles you develop as youngsters as a guide while you seek to define happiness on your own terms. Be goal-oriented, do what's important to you, but let your principles channel your actions in the right direction. As you reach your goals (and even if you fall short) the taste that's left in your mouth will be that much sweeter for having done things the right way.

Second, the inner joy that comes from knowing that you've lived up to your beliefs through your actions, is very real. I've done some things that other folks might consider stupid, but I know inside that I did them because of what I believed in, and the very thought of that makes me happy. In spite of the cost, I'd do the same things over again.

I'm going to wrap up this letter by listing the principles that have guided me in my search for happiness. I'm not saying that you have to follow them or that they guarantee happiness (they don't), but please know that they have served me well in my personal journey. Also, in spite of straying from them more than I should, each of these principles has always been willing to take me back for another try.

1. Make the most of whatever talents and circumstances God has bestowed upon you
2. Live curious
3. Be accepting of different lifestyles and beliefs
4. Recognize that there's no substitute for hard work
5. Walk like you're going somewhere
6. Be a Baller, not a bawler
7. Finish what you start
8. Hubris: Please don't do this
9. Be sure to say thank you
10. Help others on their journey
11. Don't be afraid to admit when you're wrong
12. Tell your, "loved ones" that you love them

I hope that one day when you're adults and maybe even have your own kids that you look back happily on what is written in these pages.

I love you,

Fafa

LETTER IV

WHAT PRICE FREEDOM?

Dear Nico, Bella and Vali,

As Bella wraps up her junior year of high school and starts focusing on getting into college, there's been some talk around the house about, "Freedom." Of course, the type of freedom we've been discussing is related to Bella escaping mom's watchful eye, but those conversations got me thinking about the different types of freedom that exist in the world, and the price that people pay to achieve them.

I can relate to Bella's desire to do what she wants with her life; all the years of my early adulthood were spent seeking the freedom to do the things that I deemed important. While I can say that I achieved the liberty I so aggressively chased after, I must also confess that its very pursuit taught me some lessons I hadn't anticipated. The purpose of this letter is to share those learnings with you.

Looking back, it's clear that my life-long quest for freedom started in high school. As you know, I spent my senior summer as an exchange student in Colombia. While that was an amazing journey, I also think it was the year-long process of applications, essays and interviews needed to qualify for the program that created a pent-up desire for adventure that permanently molded my way of thinking.

Proof of the above mindset can be seen in my 1980 Lynn English High School year book. Back then, students could post a motto or favorite saying under their photo, and the one I chose said it all…"Plans to live overseas." It was with that thought in mind that I left a few days after graduation for what became the first chapter in my, "Grand Adventure."

I spent the summer of 1980 in Colombia and that experience changed my life.

In terms of freedom, though, the "Aha Moment" was when my Colombian host family let me travel alone by bus from Popayán to Cali to visit some cousins of theirs. It might seem silly, but I recall the exhilaration I felt from finding the right bus in a packed terminal where no one knew who I was, or cared what I was doing.

Another defining moment came when I was studying at American International College out in Springfield, Massachusetts. When I came back from Colombia, I spent my freshman year living at home and commuting to Salem State College. It took about a month to realize that my life's purpose would be better served elsewhere, so I transferred to AIC and did my remaining three years out in western Mass.

During that time I took full advantage of my freedom, but one weekend remains vivid in my mind. It centered on a trip I took to North Adams State College, a well-known party school nestled in the Berkshire Mountains of western Massachusetts. I knew two guys from home that went there, so it was always a blast to hang out and live up to our hometown title of, "Lynn, Lynn, City of Sin."

One of the cool things about North Adams was that I sometimes hitchhiked there. It's hard to envision now, but I used to toss a few sandwiches from the AIC cafeteria into a gym bag, catch a ride down to the 91 Freeway and then thumb up the Mohawk Trail out to N. Adams. A seventy five mile journey, the Berkshires are beautiful any time, but this trip took place in the fall of my junior year in 1982.

I left after Friday lunch and my first ride took me all the way to the Mohawk Trail, letting me off near a town called Shelburne Falls. As the car pulled away, I found myself alone on a flat stretch of road, with the Deerfield River to my left and mountains all around. For just a few moments there were no cars to be seen and as corny as it sounds, I was struck by a solitary connection with Mother Earth. Honestly, it was like I was the only person in the entire universe.

I was also overcome by what I can only describe as a primeval sense of freedom.

I felt the presence of the prehistoric animals that walked the same valley floor thousands of years ago, and the Native Americans that blazed the original Mohawk Trail centuries before me. I was alone without a care in the world and I loved it. The vibe lasted but a few seconds, but I'll cherish it until the day I die.

I could go on and on with stories about unfettered freedom, but the real purpose of sharing some of my stories is to set up a more important discussion on the true price of achieving personal liberty. It turns out that there are many definitions of freedom and each one has its cost. My personal journey towards freedom picked up in earnest when I graduated college and was confronted by the real world.

The first post-college lesson I learned is that if you really want to exercise freedom, you'd better have a fruitful way of making a living. No matter what your passion may be, the simple reality is that you need to have the money to finance it. Although I've said it a million times, the message here is the same: You have to be able to compete in the marketplace in order to make money to do the things you want.

The second lesson I can share with you on personal liberties is that there's nothing "free" about freedom; sooner or later there's always going to be some sort of price to pay. I already mentioned the part about needing an income, but in addition to that troublesome reality, there's much, much more.

One of the reasons I got a job in sales after college was because I dreaded the idea being in an office five days a week. I had some "corporate" gigs during my university summers and the one thing that scared me silly was the thought of being chained to a desk for forty years. While working in sales allowed me to make money and do the stuff I wanted to do, I know that I sometimes took things a little too far.

Without going into too much detail, let's say that when it came to work during my twenties, I was more about quality than quantity. Instead of being a committed employee, I dedicated a lot of my time to partying, chasing girls, dirt-biking, mountain biking and boating. In terms of time frame, I should mention that this went on from my college graduation in 1984, until I returned to Colombia in 1992.

On the other hand, I should also point out that my twenties weren't a total vacation. First mentioned in a letter entitled, "A Tale of Two Cold Calls," please recall that I did well enough in sales to earn that job transfer to Colombia in 1992. I'll also say that I took time out from my busy Social Calendar to earn a U.S. Customs Brokers license in 1988 and an MBA from the University of Miami in 1989.

So, what's the point here? Simple. When it comes to freedom, you can't have your cake and eat it, too. You can't work twenty hours a week and expect to be CEO of a company. You can't treat work like a hobby without one day having to play career catch-up. Please know that I have had to make up for lost time and that I'm now in a mad sprint to the finish line. How that race ends has yet to be determined.

The other point is that it won't be just you that pays a price for exercising your freedom; those close to you will be impacted, too. The fact that I wasn't the best employee did harm to the people I worked for. I also had a girlfriend in my twenties and suffice it to say that I wasn't the best boyfriend, either. Later in life when I was travelling for work and was never around, it was you guys and mom that paid the price.

All of the situations I put myself in created what business people call, "Opportunity Cost." As applicable to life choices as to business situations, opportunity cost measures the consequences of choosing between alternative actions. Basically, it acknowledges that no one can do two things at the same time, and the price of choosing one path over another is the one you didn't choose.

In my twenties, I chose freedom over work, so the opportunity cost was professional advancement. In my thirties, I travelled like crazy and saw the world, but the opportunity cost was time lost with family.

In other words, when making life choices, opportunity cost is what you sacrifice when deciding on a course of action. Clearly, I fulfilled a lifelong dream of working in Latin America when I returned to Colombia. As great as it was, the opportunity cost was moving away, knowing that the time lost with my parents could never be recovered. Now that they're both gone, I know how accurate that math was.

While none of the above is intended to dissuade you from living the lives you want, I will urge you to seek balance in all that you do. Whether you're just starting out or you're in your fifties, try to seek what the ancient Greek philosopher Aristotle called, "The Golden Mean." The Golden Mean is about avoiding extremes in anything that you do and instead, trying to find a middle ground.

So, sully forward with big goals, infuse your lives with a sense of adventure and a desire to experience everything that this world has to offer. Work hard to achieve the economic freedom needed to do the things that make you happy, but be sure to find the time to be with the people that you love the most. And as opportunity knocks and you have to make big choices, do your best to calculate the real cost.

Love,
Fafa

LETTER V

THE DUMB END OF THE TAPE

Dear Nico, Bella and Vali,

My father was a carpenter by trade and he was always coming up with one-liners and Words of Wisdom that reflected the lingo of his profession. Picked up from the construction crews and blue collar bars of Boston's North Shore, some were corny, but a few were real gems. All of them have remained with me, and to this day they provide guidance and a reminder of the many conversations my dad and I shared.

One of his favorite one-liners didn't surface until I was a young man. By the time I was eighteen or so, your Uncle Dickie and I were always talking about girls and if Grampa Dick was close by he'd chime in with the same carpenter's advice. No matter who we were talking about, Grampa Dick's input was always the same, "Don't marry a girl that lives on a hill because she'll never be on the level."

After a couple of years of hearing the same joke over and over, we'd start laughing before he even said it, just because we knew it was coming. Uncle Dickie and I would be carrying on about some young lady, my dad would get that wry look on his face and the cadence would hilariously repeat itself yet again.

To this day, I can envision the scene in my mind's eye…The three of us sitting around the living room of my parent's house, me and Uncle Dickie talking about girls, my dad preparing his delivery and then the three of us howling as we recited the punchline in unison. With both Grampa Dick and Uncle Dickie gone now, I can honestly say that I'd give just about anything for one more of those silly exchanges.

Grampa Dick wasn't all jokes and he imparted a great deal of wisdom with just a few words of advice that he learned as a tradesman. Two of my favorites were his stories on what he called, "Hammer Mechanics" and the one that's stuck with me most, "The Dumb End of the Tape." Let's begin with Hammer Mechanics as it's a great lead-in to the tape story.

Back in the day, if a tradesman was good with his hands, he was known to be a, "good mechanic." This complement wasn't reserved for guys that worked on cars; a real mechanic was a generalist that could build or fix anything…a go-to-guy when something needed to be, "Done right on the job site." Grampa Dick was especially keen on this description because he was a great mechanic by birth and by training.

When my father got out of the Navy after WWII he took advantage of the G.I. Bill to study carpentry and construction at Wentworth Institute in Boston. That training, combined with God-gifted hands and a knack for math made him a natural for all things mechanical. In fact, up until the day he passed away on January 1, 2007, I can't recall a single time we had a handy man come to our house.

For example, when he bought his home at 23 Bulfinch Terrace in Lynn, MA in 1956, he remodeled the whole thing himself. The masonry for the wall that leveled off our back yard was also courtesy of Grampa Dick. Over the years any electrical, plumbing, or heating repairs got their start in my dad's toolbox.

Given his vocation, one of the few things that annoyed my father was the legion of laborers in the Lynn area that upon strapping on a tool belt, immediately called themselves a carpenter. Grampa Dick had immense respect for anyone that worked for a living, but it just irked him to see people passing themselves off as craftsmen when they hadn't put in the time or effort to legitimately do so.

And that's where the term Hammer Mechanic came from…Someone that only knew how to use one tool, but that was armed with a fundamental belief that anything could be fixed with a hammer, as long as you swung it hard enough. As you might imagine, being known as a Hammer Mechanic was not meant to flatter.

In my case, it was clear from childhood that I had no mechanical skills, so I always wondered why he brought up the story of the Hammer Mechanic so often. When I got older, he revealed that he wasn't talking about becoming a carpenter; the message was that regardless of the profession I chose, I should take advantage of whatever talent I had and work hard to be the best at my chosen field.

Over time, I learned that he would have been equally proud to see me become a plumber or an accountant, but in neither case would he tolerate a Hammer Mechanic. Be advised Nico, Bella and Vali that I will hold you to the same standard.

The "Dumb End of the Tape" story is a special one because I actually lived it first-hand. Because my father worked in and around the trades his whole life, he had an endless list of buddies that would gladly hire his two sons to join a construction crew or swing a mop.

My older brother got his first taste of hard labor with the McDonough Fence Company in the early seventies and I was introduced to the business-end of a jack hammer while working for Kelleher Construction up in Beverly, MA. It was during that time that I first encountered the dumb end of the tape.

By the time I joined Kelleher my sophomore summer of college, I had already held a number of jobs. After being a dishwasher and factory hand, I figured a construction gig would be no problem. Kelleher was close to my dad's job at the United Shoe Machinery Corporation, so we rode to work together every day for that entire summer. It was on the first day of work, as I got out of the car that he offered me the advice, "Make sure you don't stay on the dumb end of the tape your whole life."

I had no idea what he was talking about, but it didn't take long to figure out. Like any construction outfit, we were assigned to whatever jobs happened to be going on during a given time period. Over the course of that summer I dug ditches, tore down old structures, helped pour concrete foundations and paved parking lots.

As luck would have it, that first day I had the relatively easy job of being a flunky for a crew of carpenters. Basically, the carpenters were doing all of the highly-skilled finish work in a beautiful home in Beverly Farms and my assignment was to do whatever they told me. After an hour of lugging wood into the house, one of the carpenters asked me to help him take some measurements.

Another old adage that my dad always used was, "Measure twice, cut once," so I knew it was serious work when a carpenter measured for precise cuts on really expensive pieces of wood. So, I thought I was pretty important when this guy name Ray (yes, I still remember his name) peeled off a few inches from his tape measure and told me to hold it at the end of the length of wood.

My self-importance quickly faded, however, as he walked out the tape and began marking his measurements with a flat-sided carpenter's pencil. It was then I realized that Ray was doing all of the calculating and thinking, and I was the one holding, "The dumb end of the tape."

Now, to be clear, my dad instilled in me the belief that there is dignity in all types of work. He taught me that any man that is willing to get up in the morning and go to work every day on behalf of his family is worthy of another man's respect. From the get-go, I knew that his dumb end of the tape comment had nothing to do with looking down on people that worked for a living.

Quite the contrary, it is to this day that as a business executive and someone who has managed thousands of people, that I have the most empathy for, and feel the most comfortable around, the people who do the real work. It was my dad that provided me with that all-important perspective.

With the above said, Grampa Dick also believed that just because someone started out on the dumb end of the tape, it didn't mean that they had to stay there. When he picked me up that night from work, he could tell by the smile on my face that I had already discovered the meaning of his earlier advice.

We had a special laugh that evening and I have to say that the thirty minutes we spent talking on the ride home was one the most formative moments in my life.

Allow me to summarize what that conversation has meant to me:

First, from that moment I knew that if I was going to amount to anything, I was going to have to work for it. My parents were putting me through college, but beyond that, I knew that I'd have to do a lot of the heavy lifting. That was a life-changing realization because when you combine a belief in yourself with an undying willingness to work for the things you want, there is no human feeling that is more invigorating.

To that end, if there is one thing that gives me great solace is the knowledge that I never have, nor will I ever give in to life's curve balls or more importantly, the consequences of my own bad decisions and mistakes. I would urge you to soldier through life with the same mentality; it will keep you moving forward and allow you to confront whatever this world throws your way.

The second, and probably bigger lesson I got from that conversation was that no matter what I ended up doing for a living, it was my responsibility to be the best at it that I could possibly be. Grampa Dick always talked about stuff like, "Giving an honest day's work for a fair day's wages" and, "Take pride in what you do," but what he was getting at on that ride from Beverly to Lynn went much deeper.

For him, getting off the dumb end of the tape meant that a person takes whatever talent God gives him and makes the most of it. It also meant working hard at one's craft, improving a little bit every day and in the end, being able to look in the mirror and know that you put your best effort forward. Basically, the message was, "Don't go through life as a Hammer Mechanic."

While I've had my ups and downs, I'm happy to report that I've lived up to Grampa Dick's words. Even though I'm not the most "successful" or richest person in the world, I do carry the deep satisfaction of knowing that I worked hard to develop the meager talents I was given, that I achieved the goals I set for myself and most importantly, that I'm well prepared to take on my final challenges on this earth.

It's now up to you to develop the talents you've been blessed with and make the most of them. Mom and I will have lived up to our end of the bargain, but you guys have to take the baton and advance it much further up the track. That means establishing big goals for yourselves, planning a strategy to achieve them and most of all, getting down to the hard work of making your goals a reality.

It won't be easy…you'll make plenty of mistakes, and you will run the risk of being consumed by failure and disappointment. In those darkest of moments, look beyond the short-terms failures and focus on being the best person you can be. Trust me, when you look inside yourself and know that you gave your best effort, true happiness won't be far behind.

In closing, I'd like to share a great story from the artist, Pablo Picasso. It's perfect for this letter because it talks about not only being the best you can be at your life's work, but also about being your own person while you're doing it.

Much like Grampa Dick wanted to be the best mechanic, Picasso's story goes like this…"My mother said to me, 'If you are a soldier, you will become a general. If you are a monk, you will become Pope.' "Instead, I was a painter and became Picasso."

You three are my Picasso's and each of you has a blank canvas upon which you can paint your own Grand Adventure. I urge you to work in broad strokes, using only the boldest and brightest of colors.

Love,
Fafa

LETTER VI

A HARD FOUGHT "B" IS BETTER THAN AN EASY "A"

Dear Nico, Bella & Vali,

The theme of many of the letters I've written you center on achieving happiness through self-actualization. In a nutshell, self-actualization comes down to taking whatever talents and circumstances God has given you, and doing your best to reach your full potential. You don't have to be a superstar at something to self-actualize, you just need to set goals and work hard to achieve them.

An unexpected result of those letters was that they forced me to think deeply about my own experiences with self-actualization. During those times I repeatedly found myself asking the most basic of questions, "What have I gotten out of this life-long cycle of setting goals, working really hard, failing a lot and succeeding a little?" My innermost thoughts on this question is the topic of today's letter.

Needless to say, the whole idea of setting a goal is to achieve it. And while "success" is the end-game of any undertaking, there is much happiness to found in the process itself. In other words, there are few emotions that compare with the exhilaration of being in the thick of a worthy fight whose outcome has yet to be determined.

Also, as you engage in the work of reaching a goal you will soon find out how deep inside yourself you're willing to dig to make it real. There's something uniquely personal about digging deep, because you're the only person that really knows if you gave your best effort. When you're working towards a goal there's a special satisfaction that comes from knowing that win or lose, you left everything on the field.

When I think about these emotions, I can't help but recall Nicolas' six year roller coaster ride with the YMCA's Youth & Government program. We all know that when Nico was a junior at Peninsula High he won the most important election at Y&G, Youth Governor of the state of California. What we sometimes forget is that throughout his time in the program, he lost almost as many elections as he won.

I am especially sensitive to Nico's second biggest campaign, the one he lost to his political nemesis, that kid, "Riley." I remember the night of the election when Nico, mom and I were all crying in our bedroom, hugging each other. After blubbering through a reading of the famous speech by Teddy Roosevelt, "The Man in the Arena," I told Nico he had two choices.

First, he could assume the fetal position, retire from political life at age sixteen and never risk the humiliation of such a loss again. Or, he could regroup, devise a new strategy and come back even stronger the next year for the really big election, Youth Governor. And to his credit, Nico did just that, working his butt off for an entire year, devising and executing on a plan of attack.

I'm confident Nico will say that all the hard work he put into his campaigns was a source of great satisfaction. What I'll tell you is that while I'm very happy he won, I'm way prouder of the fact that Nico looked defeat straight in the eyes, doubled down at the risk of even greater despair and rallied big time. That is why I'm not only proud of Nico, I admire him for the moxy he displayed at such a young age.

Another great example of sticking with a goal is Bella's ordeal during her junior year at Palos Verdes High School. We all know that high school is a living hell in terms of preparing to apply for college, where the slightest dip in a grade or a sub-par SAT score will alter a child's future forever. Not unlike many youngsters, Bella got a little off track and while she wasn't doing badly, she could have done a lot better.

At the mid-point of junior year Bella was underperforming and needed to stage a comeback in terms of grades. Simultaneous to that, Bella had taken the ACT for the first time and came out with a less than stellar score of 27. Based on her own soul-searching (and maybe some urging from mom and dad), Bella knew that she had to either buckle down or miss getting into a college of her choice.

Overnight, Bella was hard at work on her grades and studying like crazy to jack-up her ACT score. In the end, Bella finished with straight A's and an ACT score of 32! Although that's not the highest score possible, it's the highest score Bella could get and when all is said and done, that's all that matters. A come from behind performance that no one can take away from her...outstanding work, Bella!!!

My second-to-last comment on self-actualization is that you don't necessarily have to accomplish world-shattering things to find happiness. Actually, doing small stuff can be just as gratifying, not to mention put you in a mindset that lets you strive for bigger things. Out of all the experiences I've had in my own life, there's one little-known story I fall back on when I need a little self-encouragement.

When I was studying for my MBA at U Miami in 1988-1989, one of the mandatory classes was Business Calculus. Now, we all know that none of us are math geniuses, so I was particularly worried about this class, especially since I didn't take Calculus in high school or college. After the first day, I realized that I didn't even understand the underlying Algebra and instantly knew that I was in trouble.

So, at the age of twenty six, I went and got a tutor who happened to be a very attractive, eighteen year old freshman girl. At first, I had visions of dating my tutor but those dreams got wrecked when she figured out during our second session that I was a "Math Boob" and condescendingly asked, "What kind of math classes did you take in high school and college, anyway?"

The tutoring thing tanked, but I decided that I was going to work my tail off to get a good grade. Long story short, I studied harder for that class than any other and barely got a "B". I took Business Calculus in 1988 and I still remember how happy I was to EARN that grade. Ironically, what that class really taught me had nothing to do with math; I learned that in life, a hard-fought "B" is way better than an easy "A".

More than anyone, the above tale is for Vali. At thirteen she's too young for huge goals, but I hope this story shows that small acts can have big results. Working on a goal teaches the true value of effort and it forces you to realize that nobody's going to give you anything in this life. Her qualifying for the WEB Program at school is a great example of this and will hopefully be a stepping stone to more success!

So, to wrap this letter up, I need to answer the question I started out with: What has this commitment to self-actualization and reaching my own potential really done for me? In devising an answer I'm reminded of the two main goals of my life. As unambitious as it might sound, the only things I ever wanted to do was learn to speak Spanish really well and travel the world on someone else's dime.

In the course of pursuing those goals I had major achievements and some colossal failures. For now, I'll say that for every success there were numerous missteps and self-inflicted wounds. When I look at the final tally, though, and in spite of failing along the way, I accomplished what I set out to do. And no matter what happens the rest of my life, no one can take that away from me. I like that feeling a lot.

The last thing I'll say is that my own goals have changed over time. With Nico at Vanderbilt and Bella and Vali not far behind, my greatest satisfaction comes from providing for the three of you. Nothing's changed since the first letter I wrote you when I said that a parent's job description was, "To leave the next generation poised for greater things." Mom and I continue to take that mission very seriously.

The sense of accomplishment I get from the things mom and I do to help you guys achieve your own goals feels better than any single thing I've ever done.

That same feeling of joy harkens me back to my own dad and the great feeling he must have gotten from providing for his kids, and giving each of us the opportunity to do a little bit better than he did.

In closing, as you begin your own never-ending journey towards meeting your full potential, remember the words of the author Miguel Cervantes who said, "The road is always better than the inn." Enjoy the trip; may it be both long and rich with life experiences.

Love,

Fafa

LETTER VII

LOVE AFFAIR WITH A LANGUAGE

Dear Nico, Bella and Vali,

Of all the letters I've written you, this one is especially revealing in terms of the people and events that shaped my life. As you'll quickly see, everything you read here centers on the four-decade-long love affair I've had with the Spanish language. Whereas we all know the history of how I ended up in Colombia and met mom, there's an amazing backstory that just has to be told.

I've been planning on sharing this tale for some time, but I wasn't sure how to start. Then, I came to the realization that my experiences with Spanish really do add up to a love affair. I had never thought of it that way, but like many relationships, "she" has been fickle and sometimes hard to understand. And many times, the more I pushed for answers, the more reluctant she was to give up her deepest secrets.

On the other hand, Spanish has been the one constant in my life since the age of thirteen. She's always been there for me, providing entertainment, intellectual stimulation and a sense of accomplishment like no other. And the few times I wandered off and even thought about leaving her for good, she always took me back. It's those ups and down in the relationship that I most want to convey to you.

By the time I was in the sixth grade at St. Pius V School I knew I wasn't cut out for a Catholic education. I had already begun to have doubts about religion in general and because public school junior high started in seventh grade, it was the perfect time to make a change. As you might imagine, it took some time to get your Nana Mary on board with the idea of going to public school, but she eventually gave in.

The first thing I learned about Pickering Junior High was that I'd have to study a language, with the two options being French or Spanish. In what seemed like no big deal, I recall my parents debating the issue and my mom saying, "There's way more people in Lynn speaking Spanish than French, so you're taking Spanish." And as harmless a decision as it was, that's how I was first introduced to Español.

Let's fast forward to Lynn English High School and say that my relationship with Spanish was definitely not, "Love at first sight." I wasn't a very good student in junior high, I didn't feel like I had any special talent for languages (or anything else, for that matter), but I kept plugging along. That is, until I got to the eleventh grade and met the second woman in my life that changed everything, Ms. Karen Browne.

Let me begin by saying that "Miss Browne" was an amazing educator. She taught eleventh and twelfth grade Spanish, which were the two highest levels you could get to, Spanish IV and Spanish V. I didn't really have a big interest in the language until I got to her class and she literally set the course for the balance of my life.

It's hard to say how old she was back in 1978-80, but my guess is Miss Browne was in her mid-to-late-thirties. She was a thin woman, very classy, with short blonde hair and always well dressed. Having been to her house in Marblehead for school events, we learned that her husband was a bigshot at the General Electric in Lynn and that she taught because she loved it, not because she had to.

For reasons I surmised later, Miss Browne showed an interest in me early on, perhaps seeing something in me that I didn't see in myself. Maybe it was because by the time I got to Spanish IV, I was the only kid in class that wasn't on the National Honor Society, and she felt bad for me. What I did find out for sure was that she liked me because of the way I treated three new kids that joined the class.

Sometime during junior year we had three new people arrive to class, a brother and sister duo, as well as a third, unrelated girl. All three were from Guatemala, spoke little to no English and they no doubt got thrown into Spanish because they understood what people were saying. I didn't think anything of it, but I took to talking to them, showing them around and making them feel welcome.

Well, as Miss Browne stated in a reference letter she wrote for me a few years later, the fact that I was "popular at school" (her words) and accepting of these kids sent a signal to the other students that it was OK to be nice to them. I wasn't trying to influence anyone else's behavior, I just thought it was the right thing to do.

From there, Miss Browne encouraged me to join a club that hosted foreign exchange students through an organization called, "American Field Services." AFS set up exchange programs for high schoolers around the world and Lynn English had kids coming and going from a number of countries. I joined, and she then pushed me to apply to become an exchange student over the summer of my senior year.

During my whole final year of high school, Miss Browne coached me, helped fill out paperwork and she even drove me to interviews over a series of several weekends. In the end, I was chosen to participate in the AFS program and I spent my whole senior summer in Popayán, Cauca, Colombia with a family of five. As you well know, that became the first of dozens of trips I'd make to Colombia over the years.

Karen Browne had a much greater influence over me than what I've described thus far. She taught us very well, with a heavy emphasis on learning what I still consider to be some pretty trick grammar. She showed us how to minimize a gringo accent in Spanish by placing our tongues behind our two front teeth when we spoke. To this day, people still complement me on the minimal accent I have in Spanish.

Maybe even more importantly, I didn't misbehave in high school because I didn't want to disappoint Miss Browne. Basically, I wanted to prove to her, my fellow classmates and ultimately myself that I was just as capable as the National Honor Society kids. That desire inspired me to work really hard and learn things in her class that I still use to this day.

Also, and in what turned out to be a good thing, Spanish class for junior and senior year was the last period of every day. That might not sound like much, but a lot of my friends were skipping school and/or smoking weed at lunch, so by the end of the day they were either gone or entirely spaced out. In part, I never did any of that stuff because I had Spanish last period and I didn't want to hurt Miss Browne.

Apart from my own mother and the relationship I have with mom, I'd be hard pressed to find a more influential woman in my life than Karen Browne. She was a great teacher that showed confidence in me when I didn't have any in myself. To paraphrase from the autobiography of Colin Powell when he spoke of a special teacher his daughter had, "Every child should have a Karen Browne come into their lives."

My summer in Colombia was a game changer, but before I knew it, I was back in Lynn starting my freshman year at Salem State College. Of course, I signed up for Spanish and did the same thing when I transferred out to American International College for my three remaining years of university. Overall, I took enough classes to earn a minor in Spanish from AIC and got a lot out of every class I took.

Spanish was different for me after college because for the first time in nine years I didn't have the structure of classroom study. I managed to temporarily fix that problem by finding a class at the Harvard Extension School called, "Spanish for Business." I learned quite a bit, but more importantly, my wanderings in Cambridge and Boston introduced me to the Latino corner stores in the area.

I kept going back to those little "tiendas" because they sold comic books in Spanish. This might sound like a weird way to learn, but if you think about it, comics are perfect for languages because they're all dialogue, with the added benefit of illustrations for context. I can tell you for sure that Pato Donald,

Ratón Mickey and Condorito taught me as much Spanish as any professor ever did.

I have to say that my love affair with Spanish did go through some tough years. As you will have read in another letter, I had a failed move to Puerto Rico that set me back, and I basically had a four or five year period when I was thinking about giving up on my dream of working in Latin America. Thankfully for all of us, I kept grinding, but there were a few times that I was on the brink of hanging it up.

One source of my despair during those years was the Spanish nightly news broadcast on Univision. Every night I'd come home and listen to the news anchor (the same guy that's on TV to this day), Jorge Ramos, and he spoke so fast I never understood a word he said. I studied and studied and listened intently, but every night it was the same story……nada.

And then one night I came home, turned on the TV and braced myself for another dose of disappointment. I don't consider it a miracle, but it was certainly magical because suddenly, I understood what he was saying. That was the boost I needed to get over those rough years, recommit to my relationship with Spanish and carry on. Let's call this little story my, "Jorge Ramos Moment."

It was a good thing I stuck with it, because my big chance in Latin American came in 1992 when I was working for Fritz Companies. As I've also mentioned in other letters, Fritz was setting up operations in Latin America and needed bilingual executives in each country to spearhead the operation. That's when I met Mr. Ralph Gazitua, yet another very important figure that helped to pave the road for me.

Ralph was President of Latin America for Fritz and he actually travelled all the way to Boston to interview me. I heard he loved to work out, so in addition to the interview, I took him to my gym and even invited him over to Revere Beach for a lobster role. Ralph made me an offer and within ninety days, I was on the ground in Colombia. To this day, I owe Ralph an immense debt of gratitude.

I don't know if I believe in destiny, but after seventeen years of working towards my goal of getting to Latin America, I arrived to Colombia for the second time at the age of thirty, on the same day that the 500th Anniversary of Columbus' discovery of the Americas was being celebrated. Destiny or not, it was pretty wild to see my dream come to fruition on such an important day in the region's history.

From there, as the saying goes, the rest was history. I met mom towards the tail end of my stay in Colombia and most of the time that we dated, I was back in Miami. Clearly an, "Amor de lejos, amor de pendejos" situation, we got married in November of 1994 and here we are. As a family we lived in Miami for eight years, Guadalajara for nearly four and I travelled all over Latin America, multiple times.

As I reflect on my relationship with Spanish, I'm more in love with her now than ever. It continues to bring me experiences and friendships I would never have had otherwise. It's taken me around the world, including countless trips to sixteen Spanish-speaking countries. It also brought me to mom, the second woman I've known that has truly loved and stood by me. That's a big debt to owe to a language.

Now when I think about Spanish, I focus on what it can do for you guys. I know I sound like a, "disco rayado," but here comes the advice anyway. First, be proud Latinos and show your heritage the proper respect by learning Spanish for real. You already have a huge advantage, having been around the language and in Latin America from the day each of you was born. Do not squander that foundation.

Learn the language properly and it will give back to you in ways you'll never be able to repay. By definition, language skills help you to understand other people and have empathy for their stories and experiences. I'd like to think that if a fraction of the moron politicians in D.C. could speak to "illegals" in their own language, their appreciation for their plight would increase one hundred fold.

From a practical perspective, being bilingual will make you more competitive in the workplace, too. Even though I was NEVER motivated by money in my pursuit of Spanish, a side benefit has been that I made a lot more cash than I would have, had I been just another English-only White Boy. My hope for each of you is that upon mastering the Spanish language, you become more competitive by learning a third one.

For all of the gifts that Spanish has given me, the greatest has been finding your mother and having each of you as my children. I'm proud of you for a lot of reasons, but I'm just happy to have been blessed with my beautiful, "American Babies." You are indeed the product of the Age of Globalization and a living payoff from a lot of hard work, good luck and some very special people that helped me along the way.

As the years go by and your own lives unfold, please don't ever lose your blood connection with the Latin culture and its mother tongue. God knows that given all the turmoil around immigration and the plot to "Make America White Again," the country needs people like you to stand tall and defend those that can't defend themselves. Now there's something that would make me really proud.

All my love,
Fafa

LETTER VIII

A TALE OF TWO COLD CALLS

Dear Nico, Bella and Vali,

My next letter to you is based on an article I published a while back that got quite a heartfelt response from many of the people who read it. Ironically, I wrote the article with you three in mind because it's really not about salespeople at all. What's it's really about is setting goals that are hard to achieve.

You'll see that I had you guys in mind because I wrote the piece in a way that reveals a bit about our family history, the events that led to my living in Colombia and ultimately, how I met mom. To this day, I marvel at the good fortune I had, all of which was based on my own willingness to, "get uncomfortable" in the pursuit of my goals.

So, the theme of this letter is a simple one: Step into your discomfort zone and you just might find things that make you really happy. I know that sounds contradictory, but it's true. The below might help to understand why…

…Whenever I see an article or post on sales people making cold calls, l always stop to read it. Having started my own career in shipping as an Account Rep, it's just fascinating to learn how younger sales folks approach the dreaded act of, "Knocking on doors."

While acknowledging that social media now offers less painful ways to find prospects, I'm here to say that in sales, and more importantly life in general, the cold call is an essential tool for anyone seeking "success" in this world.

Back when I started selling international shipping services in Boston in the late eighties, there weren't many options for identifying potential customers. Basically, there was the telephone, letters and cold calling. Long before a sales person could stalk someone on LinkedIn, things often came down to working my sales territory building by building. Unfortunately, that meant dealing with a lot of rejection.

Although painful, cold calling taught me a couple of lessons. First, there's no "art" to cold calling; it's a mindset that focuses on a positive outcome in the midst of failure and humiliation. It's funny now, but just writing this article conjures up visions of the many receptionists that clearly enjoyed tossing me from their lobbies.

The other thing I learned is that cold calling isn't about occasionally stepping outside your comfort zone; it's about repeatedly stepping into your discomfort zone. And as you gradually develop the Nirvana-like "thick skin" that sales gurus talk about, that's when a string of cold calls turn into a pattern, which when practiced consistently, becomes an unwavering habit.

And sometimes, it's that habit-born mental toughness that will literally change your life. Here are two cold calls that dramatically changed mine.

Back in 1991, I was working in sales for Fritz Companies, which at the time was one of the country's top shipping companies. I loved the job, but my goal was to work in Latin America and I knew that if I was going to get there, I'd have to close some big deals. In retrospect, it was that focus on a larger objective that pushed me to make cold calls when it would have been a lot easier to go hide out at McDonald's (there were no Starbucks back then…lol).

One day, I came across a building in an industrial park north of Boston that had a sign out for a new tenant, New England Bio Labs. As it turns out, this firm was in the bio-tech industry and was exporting hundreds of shipments a month all over the world. That cold call led to a meeting and after a few months of work, we got the business.

New England Bio Labs was the big score I needed, but it was by pure luck that not long after that, Fritz Co. started advertising for job openings in South America. And as God as my judge, it was within ninety days of applying that I was on the ground in Bogota, Colombia with all of my worldly possessions stuffed into two duffle bags.

While there were other factors that helped me along, I know that if it hadn't been for that one cold call, my Grand Adventure would have stalled or more likely, never materialized.

The job in Colombia was a Jack-of-All-Trades position with a focus on sales development. Right after arriving in 1992, I read in the, "El Tiempo" newspaper that British Petroleum had made a huge oil discovery at a site called, "La Cusiana."

The volumes of cargo that flow into a project of that size are gold for a logistics company, so I immediately went to my local boss to express an interest in taking a run at it. He quickly informed me that he had, "the highest contacts possible at BP" and that I should back off.

I let a few weeks go by and after not hearing anything from El Jefe, I inquired again. Based on the B.S. answer he gave me, I ignored him and gave it a shot myself. Now, bearing in mind that the well-defended lobbies of Latin America are hard to just waltz into, I had to start with a phone call. My Spanish was just OK at the time, so you can imagine how nervous I was as I dialed the phone.

Much to my relief, the phone was answered by a gringo named Roger Bennett who had just moved to Colombia from Houston. In spite of the fact that Mr. Bennett had never heard of my Colombian boss, he was the Shot Caller and a man who was very happy to have someone to speak English with. Fast forward nearly nine months to the day from that first call and Fritz was awarded a multi-million dollar shipping contract. That moment changed my life in ways I never would have imagined.

First, I met mom in Colombia and we've been blessed with our three, "American Babies." Second, I made friends with some great guys that still endure, each of them a tribute to the swashbuckler mentality we shared as younger men.

Third, the BP deal served as a springboard for me to reach professional heights I had never envisioned. Overall, I spent thirteen of the best years of my life in Latin America, none of which would have been possible without those two extraordinary cold calls.

Even though these two stories took place in a business setting, this article isn't just about sales people knocking on doors. More than anything, they're intended to serve as a metaphor for the overarching belief that in the end, life is one big cold call.

If you think about it, any goal that is worth pursuing is going to force you to step into your discomfort zone. Equally true is the fact that, the harder you push against the margins of your own fear, the ballsier you become. Now that's a Nirvana we should all seek.

So, I hope my message is clear: Don't let short-term fears turn your life into a series of, "What if's." Whether it's that attractive boy that you're afraid to talk to at school, an unlisted house you want to buy or an out-of-reach job, it might just be a "Cold Call" that carries the day.

And at the moment of truth when you have ten reasons to cut and run, just remember that rejection is fleeting, but regrets are permanent. Regardless of the outcome, you'll be a stronger person for having made the effort.

Love,
Fafa

LETTER IX

LEARNING FROM OUR MISTAKES (OR NOT)

Dear Nico, Bella and Vali,

I hope that you remember one of my first letters in which I talked about what most parents want for their kids, and that they almost always say the same thing, "I just want them to be happy." Ask the same parents what else they want for their kids and it's likely, "I hope they learn from my mistakes." You've heard this from me, too, so it shouldn't be hard to figure out what this letter is about.

The big thing about kids learning from a parent's mistakes is that the adult has to share those blunders in the first place. Moms and dads can do some pretty stupid stuff that not only harms themselves, but their kids, too. With the risk of self-embarrassment so high, that's probably why many parents find it easy to say, "Learn from my mistakes," but they rarely go so far as to share any painful memories.

In the spirit of opening up, I'm going to tell you two very important stories. In the first, I learned a lesson as a teen that saved me from a major tragedy a few years later. The second was much less successful because I repeated a mistake at the age of fifty that I should have avoided based on a similar experience I had in my twenties. It is my profound wish that you get something out of both of these stories.

When I was sixteen years old I took a trip with your Uncle Johnny's younger brother Kevin to visit him and my sister Kate in New Jersey. Johnny and Kate lived off the highway, down a dirt road that was lined by trees. I remember Kate having a "Rambler," one of those car models you only see now on TV shows. I also recall bugging Kate and Johnny to the point that, against their better judgement, they let Kevin and I take a spin in the Rambler down to the end of the dirt road.

I drove, and all was fine until we had to turn around and go back to the house. When I nearly finished the three-point turn I goosed the gas and the car took off. I hadn't totally straightened out the wheel, so we started angling off the road. All I had to do was take my foot off the gas and everything would've been fine, but instead I panicked, kept it on the pedal and drove head-on into a giant oak tree.

The impact was so sudden that I hit my forehead off the steering wheel and snapped back in time to see Kevin's head go through the windshield. It was obvious from the get-go that he was hurt badly, with a major laceration just over his eye, but under the eyebrow. I had a pretty good cut on the right side of my forehead, but was completely lucid.

Kevin somehow remained conscious and we managed to walk back to the house. I'll never forget the look on Johnny's face when we got close enough for him to see what was going on. We got to the E.R. and Kevin survived, but with a bad scar. I carry the guilt of that crash to this day and forty years later, I still wish I hadn't tried to act so cool. As you might imagine, I learned an important lesson that day.

Since then, I've tried to show the utmost respect for the power of an automobile. You guys always make fun of me for how slow I drive, but it all comes from wanting to be in control of the car. I've seen what an instant's panic can do and believe me, you never want to find yourself in that position. Please have respect for the road and never, ever drive with anyone who's not in control.

Six years after the car accident, I graduated college in 1984 and was living with my brother in a, "Three Family" at 8 Eutaw Avenue in Lynn, MA. I had decided to work construction for the summer before moving to Puerto Rico (more on that later) and was tooling around in a $500 car that your Uncle Dickie bought me for graduation. One night after work I was hurrying up to my parent's house for some dinner.

I jumped in my car and started flying down Eutaw Avenue. To give you an idea of the scene, the thing you have to understand about Eutaw Ave is that it runs in a straight line for about a half mile, all of which is packed with the same "Three Decker" style apartment buildings as the one we lived in. With cars parked on both sides of the street, there was no more than twenty feet across for a car to drive.

Right after I took off, I reminded myself to slow down and I decelerated from fifty down to around twenty miles an hour. And it wasn't three seconds from my slowing down that a little kid darted out from in between the parked cars and ran in front of me. He couldn't have been more than three or four years old and when he saw me coming, he froze, much like I had done in New Jersey six years earlier.

I had slowed down enough to avoid doing major damage, but I still gave the little guy a, "love tap" with my front end. I can still see him in the middle of the street, blonde hair, t-shirt and shorts, wobbling back and forth like a dazed boxer. He didn't go down, but he was visibly shaken and started crying the second he saw his mom come flying off the porch to grab him. He was fine, but I was shaking like a leaf.

I know to this day that if I hadn't slowed down, I would have killed that kid. While the accident I caused with Kevin was horrible, the lesson I took from it saved another person's life. Had that little boy died, I'm quite sure the emotional burden would have been too much and my life would have spiraled completely out of control. While a painful lesson to learn, I'm glad I didn't make the same mistake twice.

At the end of that same summer I took a big step towards my dream of working in Latin America and moved to Puerto Rico. I didn't have a job and didn't know a soul, but I bought a one-way ticket in September of 1984 and off I went. My only real plan was to get settled and start looking for a job in international sales.

When I got to Puerto Rico, I took an apartment in San Juan in an area called, "Isla Verde." It was close to all the hotels, so I got a job working nights at the, "Condado Plaza Holiday Inn." The gig was working as a host in a theatre where they did nightly cabaret shows, seating people that came in off the cruise ships.

This was the perfect deal because there were good tips and it kept my days open for job seeking.

I wasn't on the job for long when my boss decided to transfer me to be the doorman at one of the hotel bars, a little joint called, "La Posada" (yes, I still remember the name). The problem with this transfer was that it was unbelievably boring, had no tips and ran until five o'clock in the morning. When I got the news, I let me ego get the best of me, got all pissy and quit on the spot.

In the short time that all this transpired, I had sent out a bunch of resumes, but hadn't gotten any bites. I was pretty butt-hurt from the whole La Posada incident, but I lingered around for another couple of weeks, with my spirits worsening by the day. Cutting to the chase, I gave up on my dream way too soon, put my tail between my legs and went whimpering back to Massachusetts.

In the end, everything turned out fine with my Latin America goal, but I'm still haunted by the fact that I gave up on P.R. too fast. I found out just how quickly it was when a few weeks after returning home, my ex-landlord forwarded me a letter. It was from one of the companies I'd reached out to, Pfizer, and they wanted to interview me. I sometimes wonder how that would have turned out, had I stuck around.

The obvious lesson here is that I should have never let my ego get the best of me. I should have gone to Human Resources, stated my case and then made a decision in a calm frame of mind. Instead, I let my boss get to me and I ended up screwing myself. The ancient Greeks had a name for foolish pride, "Hubris." It's been the cause of many a downfall, and I was no exception.

That's a lesson that should have served me well, but thirty years later I did the same thing all over again. Nico and Bella are old enough to remember that in 2012 I took a job as President of the ocean transportation division of a company called, "Pacer International." While I take full responsibility for my actions and the harm it did to the family, there's a history there that I'd like to share with you.

First, Pacer was headquartered in Dublin, OH and was run by a bunch of older white dudes that were (mostly) a bunch of redneck, racist, homophobes. The head bigot was the CEO and someone I'd had problems with from the get-go. Honestly, I should have known better, because the same guys that hired me had screwed over the man I replaced. I had no reason to think that they'd treat me any different.

After a few face-to-face beefs with the CEO, he went behind my back and hired a new division president, who in turn, demoted me to VP of Sales. As it turns out, I knew the new guy from my previous life at Fritz Companies and didn't think much of him, either (is there a pattern forming here?). Basically, he was full of the same smug, White Privilege attitude the other Pacer idiots so proudly displayed.

I worked out of the Long Beach office for Pacer, so most of the interaction I had with new my boss was by phone. He quickly reconfirmed that he was still a sneak and a liar, so I informed him during our last conversation that I preferred to exit the business. He was disrespectful during the entire call, but when he laughed in response to something I said, I lost it, got all pissy and quit (again).

There's no doubt I was going to resign, so that's not the point. However, if I had kept my cool and exited like a professional, my contract would have paid me for an extra six months. Because I flipped out and quit over the phone, I sacrificed the six month's pay and had no job. The stupidity of my actions was bad enough, but making the same mistake as I did in Puerto Rico weighed heavily on me.

Although you guys didn't see it, this mistake put a burden on us financially. We survived, but not before having to dig into savings to cover our (considerable) expenses. As far as work goes, I had to start over again with our company, Trade Facilitators, and that wasn't easy, either. I'll say for the record that without mom's support (and patience with her maniac husband), I don't know what I would have done.

What we did do was work together and once we realized that we were on our own, devised a strategy, and went to work. Mom helped big time with Trade Facilitators and has since gotten her Real Estate Broker's license, too. The company has done well and along with some other good luck, we've emerged just fine. Even so, I'll go to my grave knowing that, "Pacergate" was a really stupid move.

I hope that my opening up about some painful memories serves to help you in the future. You'll surely make your own mistakes, and that's OK. What's not OK is repeating them and shafting yourself at the expense of those you love. So, whatever you do, don't let your foolish pride get the best of you. Whenever you feel that pride boiling up, just repeat the following: "Hubris. Please don't do this."

Avoiding the pitfalls of foolish pride is a big part of life, so please do learn from my mistakes.

Love,
Fafa

My mom and dad, Richard H. and Mary E. Gardner on their wedding day at St. Pius V Church in Lynn, MA, March 25, 1951. Best man was Frankie Lowry, Grampa Dick's best friend since childhood and the bridesmaid was my mom's sister, Aunt Ruthie.

This is the house my parents bought in 1956 for $8,000 at 23 Bulfinch Terrace, Lynn, MA. Trained as a carpenter and tradesman, my dad remodeled the entire place himself.

The house at 23 Bulfinch Terrace circa 1990. "The Terrace" was an awesome place to grow up and my parents made a great life there for me, Uncle Dickie and Aunt Kate.

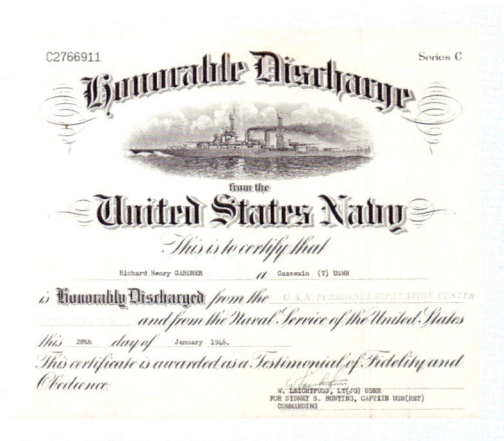

This is the birth certificate of my dad's father. It's actually one of several that I found after my dad's passing; the others say he was born in Philadelphia, Lynn and even Ireland! Clearly an "American" of dubious origins, I'm almost positive that he was born in Canada and that he came to the U.S. via less-than-official means!!!

This is me at age five in 1967, having some cereal in between playing ball. This is the same table where I asked my mom at age fourteen if I was a "mistake". Her answer, "You weren't a mistake, you were a pleasant surprise", permanently changed my world view.

Grampa Dick's Honorable Discharge from the U.S. Navy in 1946. Your grandad joined the Navy at seventeen, did Boot Camp at the Great Lakes and served in San Francisco, Norfolk and Honolulu. Influenced by his Navy days, my dad loved to captain his own boat and be out on the water with his boys.

47

All photos and documents courtesy of the Gardner Family.

This is me when I was an eighteen year old Exchange Student in Popayán, Cauca, Colombia in 1980. That trip changed my life and set me on a path that truly has been a, "Grand Adventure".

The 1979 Lynn English High School Junior Prom with me (left) and two of my closest friends, Danny Scioletti (center, RIP) and Billy Finnigan. We hung around together until I left Lynn in 1992, and I consider Bill one of my few real friends to this day.

This is "Leroy," the dog I had from the time I was thirteen until his passing circa 1990. This picture is in the living room of my parents' home, but Leroy had to come live with my brother and me after chasing the mail man up a tree one too many times!

This picture was taken on New Year's Day, either 1981 or 1982. I remember it was New Year's Day because the night before we got jumped at a party up in Ipswich, MA and I ended up with several stitches in my eye (look closely, I'm second from the left). L-R are my good friends, Billy Finnigan, Scott Finnigan and AJ Yanakakis.

This is the day my parents dropped me off at American International College in Springfield, MA (1981). I did my freshman year at Salem State College and transferred out to AIC after my mom threw me out for not following house rules. Even though she gave me the boot, Nana Mary cried like a baby when we said goodbye.

This is my 1984 graduation party from AIC, held at the Hibernian Hall in West Lynn, MA. That's me on the left, with Uncle Dickie, Aunt Kate, my mom and dad. That was the same summer I moved in with my brother at 8 Eutaw Ave in Lynn. We remained roommates until I left for Colombia for the second time in 1992.

This is my dad at the helm of the notorious vessel, the 'Qua 'Na in 1984. Grampa Dick bought the boat with Uncle Dickie and we used to go diving for lobsters off the coast of towns like Nahant, Beverly and Salem.

This is the three-family house my brother bought at 8 Eutaw Ave in Lynn around 1983. We lived in the first floor apartment and conducted our bachelor operations from there until moving to 36 Den Quarry Road a few years later.

Two of my students from the East Boston Education Center in 1986. This was first teaching job I ever had, instructing the GED to students from Central America and Cambodia. I've taught and lectured on four continents, but the most gratifying experience I ever had was helping those young people get a new start in the United States.

A photo of me in class at the East Boston Adult Education Center (1987). The "school" was actually in the basement of a converted three-decker home in the heart of, "Eastie".

This is me in downtown Amsterdam on the first international business trip I ever took (1986). I was working for a shipping company called "OceanAir" at the time, which was one of the most formative professional periods in my career.

This was from my mom's birthday party, August 12, 1989. That's Aunt Kate on the left, me, Uncle Dickie, Nana Mary and Grampa Dick. The family moments we spent together from the time I graduated college in 1984 until I left for Colombia in 1992 were some of the best ever.

49

My parents spent every winter in Naples FL, from 1988 until they couldn't travel any more. This is the, "Gardner Five" in front of the condo in Naples around 1995.

This is from the days of visiting my parents in Naples, FL, circa 1992. That's cousin Zack and Uncle Johnny on the left, cousins Brooke and Matt, and Auntie Kate on the right.

This is one of the earliest photos of mom and me, taken in Miami around 1993. If I hadn't been transferred to Bogota in 1992, mom and I never would have met and our amazing journey as a family never would have happened.

This is a picture with Grampa Dick at my going away party at my sister's house in Marblehead, MA, right before I left for Colombia in the fall of 1992. Whenever I ran into my dad's friends around Lynn they all used to say how much I looked like him. He was a handsome devil, wasn't he?

More great times from, "Back in the Day," at my sister's house in Marblehead, circa 1992. Nana Mary on the left, Uncle Art (aka, "Don Arturo"), Auntie Kate with Zachary and Matt, Grampa Dick standing up, Uncle Dickie, me and Brooke.

This is our wedding picture from November 19, 1994, taken outside the church on the outskirts of Bogota. Mom was stunning that day; in fact my Uncle Tommy always said she, "looked just like Grace Kelly."

50

Grampa Dick, me and Patricia on the balcony of our first apartment in Aventura, Florida, 1997.

The church in Aventura, Florida on the day of Nico's christening, circa 1998

I had a chance to pay my parents back for all they'd done for me by inviting them on some fun outings. This is mom and Nana Mary at the South Beach Marina in Miami Beach, FL after a great day of fishing in 1997.

Mom and my mother on the high seas fishing out of the South Beach Marina.

This is the first house mom and I ever bought together in Aventura Lakes, FL (circa 1998). Mentioned in my first letter to you guys, it was out in front of this house on New Year's Day 2000 that my big, "Millennium Question" was answered.

Nico at age one playing the Colombian drum and guitar at the Aventura apartment in 1999. We still have that drum and break it out at Christmas every year when we do, "La Novena."

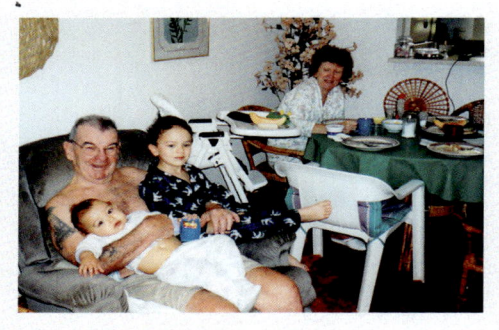

Nico and Bella with Grampa Dick and Nana Mary having breakfast at the Naples, FL condo. My parents loved being with you guys and it was such a blast to cruise over Alligator Alley from Aventura to Naples to visit them.

This is the entire Gardner side of the family in Naples, FL in 2003. L-R me, mom, Nana Mary, Grampa Dick, Bella, Uncle Dickie, cousin Zackie (back row), Nico, cousin Brooke, cousin Matt (back row), Uncle Johnny and Aunt Kate.

Nico and Bella at the beach in Mazatlán, Mexico, 2002. This was right after we moved to Mexico and was the first vacation we took together there. The look of pure happiness on both your faces amazes me to this day!

This is one of my favorite pictures of me and Bella, taken at a restaurant in Guadalajara in 2002. My mom always said that Bella was, "a beautiful child" and she was right!

Nico and Bella in San Miguel de Allende, Mexico, 2005. When we got home from this trip I got the call from my mom saying that my dad had been diagnosed with esophageal cancer. I was back in Lynn the very next day.

Mom's family at her parents' 50th wedding anniversary in Bogota. Front row, Abuelita Nora and Abuelito Humberto. Back row, Tia Natalia, Tio Sergio and Maria Patricia Serna de Gardner.

The generosity of your abuelitos is legendary; this is the Latin side of the clan at Disney World in 2009.

This is by far my favorite picture of Nico, Bella and Vali as youngsters. Taken during one of the many summers the family spent in Colombia, this time in 2009.

We moved to Los Angeles from Guadalajara on July 4, 2005. This picture was on the first day of school in 2005 in the house we were renting. Check out the look on Vali's face…she can't stop looking at me!!!

The entire Serna side of the family on yet another cruise sponsored by the abuelitos, circa 2009.

Nico, Bella and Vali at Bella's First Communion, 2010.

Vali, "The Baby" at age four.

Los abuelitos Nora and Humberto with the grandchildren, 2012. Front row, Sebastian, Bella, Sammy, Maria Jose, Vali. Back row, Sophia and Nico.

The Gardner/Serna crew at Bella's First Communion, 2010.

This is from the famous Road Trip we took in 2008 to Vegas, Utah and Arizona. Zion, Bryce Canyon and the Grand Canyon were amazing!!!

Family outing in Beverly Hills in 2006. Front row: Sammy, Tia Natalia, Vali and Bella. Back row: Patricia, Danny, Nico and Abuelita Nora.

My father's birthday party on July 31, 2006 at my brother's house in Lynn, MA. Grampa Dick was battling cancer at the time and he passed away five months later on January 1, 2007. L-R Fafa, Aunt Kate, Grampa Dick, Nana Mary and Uncle Dickie.

TELEPHONE 595-1620

LYNN ENGLISH HIGH SCHOOL
LYNN, MASSACHUSETTS 01902

ALVIN R. TAGNEY
PRINCIPAL

ALFRED E. BRESNAHAN
VICE-PRINCIPAL

February 6, 1981

To Whom It May Concern:

    It is a pleasure to recommend Dan Gardner for a foreign studies program. It is an area for which he is very well suited. Dan was an outstanding student in Spanish. In his classwork, he demonstrated intelligence, creativity, and humor as well as excellent application of what he had learned and was eager to learn more. He is extremely reliable, conscientious, and honest.

    I, his Spanish teacher, appreciated Dan's initiative in making a special effort to talk to the Hispanic students in class, two of whom spoke no English. He helped them to feel welcome and to adjust to their new culture. This is especially noteworthy because there exists a strong prejudice directed toward the Hispanics at this school. Because he was popular with and respected by his schoolmates, others followed his example. Dan has that individualistic quality that is unusual for a popular teenager: he is not afraid to disagree with the "crowd" for what he believes to be right and fair. He is a warm, caring, and sensitive individual.

    In a first interview, Dan appears somewhat reserved, due to nervousness, which makes him seem less outgoing and less articulate that he genuinely is. He does adapt readily to new situations and has a delightful sense of humor. He just needs time to "size things up."

    Because of the aforementioned characteristics, Dan was selected to participate the the American Field Service exchange program. In Colombia, Dan adapted well quickly. He participated fully in his foreign family's activities and became well acquainted with Colombian culture and people. He proudly returned at the end of the summer with a working fluency in Spanish. We made a wise decision in choosing Dan as an ambassador of American youth. This experience was a springboard for his interest in pursuing studies in foreign affairs. We are confident that he will continue to excel in his studies and his chosen career.

Karen H. Browne, Spanish Teacher

Karen H. Browne

Marilyn J. Needham, AFS Advisor

Marilyn J. Needham

This is a letter of recommendation that my high school Spanish teacher, Ms. Karen Browne did for me in 1981. I wrote lovingly of Ms. Browne in the letter, "Love Affair with a Language." As I said in that letter, every child should have a teacher like Ms. Browne.

I was an avid fisherman in my younger days, both fresh and saltwater. This is from a trip with my dad and brother, I was around nineteen years old. We were fishing off the coast of Gloucester, MA; that's me holding a codfish.

Circa 1984 from a fishing trip off the coast of Nahant, MA. As you can probably tell, things got a little crazy that day. I'm in the front holding a blue fish, Uncle Dickie is behind me, to the left.

Grampa Dick and me at the South Beach Marina in 1997 after a spectacular day of fishing. You'll note I'm sporting my full U Miami memorabilia!

This is me in 2007 on an overnight fishing trip out of San Diego. At age 45, I'm hold a yellowfin tuna that put up one hell of a fight.

"My Pally Vali" in 2008 (age three) with Mickey Mouse. One of the best parts of living in Southern California was the ability to go to Disney whenever we wanted!!!

The madman, "Teddy" circa 2015. The sudden and tragic loss of, "The Ted" should serve as a reminder of how fragile life really is and how everything can change with a single phone call.

My "Beautiful American Babies" at Squaw Valley, Thanksgiving 2018. You've all grown up so quickly, but wherever you go in this world, don't ever forget who you are, or where you came from.

One of our favorite places in all of California, Squaw Valley. Taken on Thanksgiving 2018, Dad, Nico (age 20), Bella (age 17), mom and Vali (age 13). California has been so good to us and provided priceless memories!!!

The Fritz Manager's meeting in Arizona, circa 1992. That's me on the right with my good friend and fellow Seeker, Ronnie Jordan. My years at Fritz had a huge influence on my career and I'm forever grateful for the time I spent there.

LETTER X

9/11

Dear Nico, Bella and Vali,

As a kid, it was many-a-time that I heard a grown-up say, "I'll always remember where I was when I first heard that President Kennedy had been shot." I wasn't yet two years old when JFK got killed, so I have no memory of that. Unfortunately, the tragedy of 9/11 was a different story and I know exactly where I was when I found out about it. This letter recounts how 9/11 forever altered our family trajectory.

When 9/11 happened we had already been living in Miami for seven years. It was the ideal location because I was working as Vice President of Latin America for Exel Global Logistics and it was the best city to travel from for the weekly trips I made to places like Argentina, Brazil and Mexico. Miami is also half-way between Boston and Bogota, so it was great for travelling to see our respective families.

I'll never forget that 9/11 happened on a Tuesday because I used to teach night school on Monday's at Florida International University. Because I was travelling so much, I'd either take a red-eye flight from MIA after class or, depending on where I was going, take an early flight Tuesday morning. I taught my normal class on Monday 9/10/01 and the next morning I was on a 7:00 a.m. flight to Mexico City.

Normally, I'd get excited about travelling, but this trip was different. A few months prior I had hired a new Country Manager for Mexico and he turned out to be a disaster. The only reason I was travelling to Mexico City that day was to fire him, and it wasn't something I was looking forward to. Little did

I know that when I left that Tuesday, I'd come back to a country that would never be the same.

I didn't hear a thing about 9/11 until we landed in Mexico City. The first sign that something was wrong was when a guy walking up the jet-way in front of me answered his cell phone and let out the strangest cry. I had never heard a sound like that before and honestly, I've not heard anything like it since. As I walked into the total chaos of the terminal, it didn't take long to figure out what had happened.

Like the hundreds of other people in the terminal, I stood staring at a restaurant TV screen until I could get a handle on what was happening. I could have stayed there all morning, but I wanted to get to the Exel office as quickly as possible to check on your Uncle Johnny. He's retired now, but as you know, Johnny was a pilot for Delta Airlines and I had no idea of his whereabouts.

Because we were in the cargo business, the Exel office was literally across the street from the airport and I made it there without incident. I eventually got in touch with my sister Kate and confirmed that Johnny was OK, and was then able to move on to the original reason for my trip. As hard as it may be to believe, I fired the Country Manager in the conference room, with 9/11 playing on a TV in the corner.

What you guys might not remember is that Bella was supposed to be christened that coming Saturday. Born on February 17, 2001, she was the perfect age for her baptism and the plan was to have both sets of grandparents fly in for the party. Of course, flights in and out of the U.S. were cancelled and I wasn't even sure when or how I'd get home. For all those reasons, we decided to postpone the baptism.

From the day of my arrival in Mexico on the Tuesday that was 9/11, it took me nearly a week to get home. With my flight back to Miami long-since nixed and not a lot of options, I felt an overwhelming need to get home. Even though it was seventeen years ago, I remember the details of that trip like it was yesterday.

My return started with a domestic flight up to Monterrey where Exel had another office.

I had no idea what to do after getting to Monterrey, but luckily our Branch Manager, and a friend to this day named Alvaro Barbosa picked me up and we devised a plan. The next morning, we drove about two and half hours up to Nuevo Laredo at the U.S. border. By then, some U.S. domestic flights had resumed, so the plan was to cross into Laredo, Texas and figure out how to get home from there.

The eeriest part about the whole trip was when Alvaro dropped me off and I walked across the border. I had been to Nuevo Laredo many times and there was always a line at U.S. Immigration, but that morning there wasn't a soul, and I cruised through. When I got to the U.S. side, the only real motion came from a U.S. flag that in spite of being at half mast, stood vigilant over a wounded nation.

Things sped up a bit from there, all with a little bit of luck and a huge courtesy from American Airlines. Whereas I was able to buy a ticket in Nuevo Laredo for an American Eagle flight up to Dallas, I still had no way of getting from DFW to MIA. When I got to Dallas airport I checked the outbound flights and found one that was going to Buenos Aires, via Miami.

In the midst of so many people trying to get flights, I went up to the Buenos Aires counter and explained my situation. I think the fact that I was an Executive Platinum customer of American Airlines helped my case, but I'm forever grateful to the lady at the counter who said to me, "Just get on, sit wherever you can in Economy and be sure to get off in Miami." And that's how I got home, some five days after 9/11.

Honestly, once I got home the balance of the weekend was a blur…I guess people were just in shock, myself included. I do remember I had to go to work that Monday morning, as well as teach again on Monday night. Work was a mess, with cargo being delayed all over the region from the cancelled flights and backlogs of freight. What stuck in my mind though, was that Monday night class.

One thing I didn't mention about the class I taught at FIU was that to my recollection, I was the only native born gringo in the whole group. That wasn't unusual because my class was part of a Masters in International Business program, and most everyone was from Latin America or Europe. Regardless of where everyone was from, we bonded that night and lamented our devastating loss.

As you know, I've been an adjunct professor my whole adult life and I've always put a lot of effort into my classes. I don't know if I was inspired, heartbroken for the families that lost so much on 9/11 or both, but the balance of that semester was a tour de force. In some strange way, I guess I wanted to show my students that the U.S. was still a great place to come and learn, and I poured myself into every lecture.

9/11 was a big blow for most everyone in the U.S., but after a while, day-to-day life started to take back over. That certainly was not the case for the Gardner family because out of the tragedy that was 9/11 our lives changes dramatically, and all for the better. It was about halfway through that fall semester that a call came for Exel headquarters in London to share some important news with me.

Among other things, 9/11 wreaked a lot of havoc on economies around the world. Latin America was no different and our operations suffered pretty badly. At the time, sixty percent of our business was with electronics manufacturers in Mexico and Brazil, with large offices in Guadalajara, Manaus and São Paulo.

The call was from my British boss at the time, a guy named Stephen Chipping. Basically, he told me that our Mexican operation was bleeding money and that I had to go there and fix it, in person. More of an instruction than a request, the original plan was to stay there for a year and then return to Miami. Family history shows that we lived in Guadalajara, Jalisco, Mexico for just over three years.

Vali wasn't born yet, so the crew was me, mom, Nico and Bella. I got there first, landing in GDL on January 3, 2002. I stayed by myself for three months while mom got our affairs in order. When everyone was finally together, it was early Spring of 2002…Nico was four and Bella was just over a year old. From there, our Grand Adventure in Mexico flourished.

I won't bore you with the work details, but we were able to overcome all of our problems and grow the business big time. Over the course of my time in Mexico, we not only opened up offices across the country in places like Aguascalientes and Queretaro, but we built up our South American operation, as well. Along the way, I made friends and professional relationships that endure to this very day.

For you guys, it was pretty amazing, too. You not only lived like kings in the private mountainside community of, "Bugambilias," but also took vacations in places like Mazatlán and Puerto Vallarta. Since mom's brother Sergio was living outside of Mexico City in Toluca, we got to see your three cousins a lot, as well. A visit from my mom, along with visits from mom's parents made things even better.

Sadly, of all the great trips we took, the one that stands out for me is when we drove to San Miguel de Allende for the weekend. I still have a beautiful picture of Nico and Bella from that trip, but it was that same weekend I got the call from home to say that my dad was diagnosed with cancer of the esophagus. We'll deal with that in another letter, but that was a big blow and the low point of my time in Mexico.

At the other end of the emotional spectrum, Vali was born at the tail end of our Mexico Experience, on April 8th, 2005. That was a whole other adventure because we actually went back to Miami, rented a condo for three months, had Vali and moved back to Mexico. That had to have been some kind of record because Vali was less than a month old when she got her first passport!!!

Of the thirty years I've worked in international trade and the thirteen I spent in Latin America, I have to say that without question, Mexico was the highlight of my career. We resurrected a business that was on the brink of failure, spent amazing times together as a family, Nico did Pre-K, kindergarten and first grade there, and as a family out on its own in the post-9/11 world, we stuck together.

When I think back on those blessed times, it pains me to think that none of it would have happened had it not been for the deaths of so many people on 9/11. If it weren't for 9/11, we would likely never have left Miami and I would have kept working in Latin America. Had it not been for our business success in the region, we never would have been transferred to Los Angeles, where we have also been blessed.

The list goes on and on, but Nico wouldn't have become Youth Governor of California, mom maybe wouldn't have become a Real Estate agent and none of us would have had the opportunity to see the beauty that is California. From Big Bear to Mammoth, San Diego, the Bay Area, Napa, Yosemite, Tahoe and Squaw Valley, we've been blessed to live in the great state of California.

With all that said, I feel a weird sense of guilt about how our lives turned out after 9/11. I know it wasn't our fault, but while we prospered in the 9/11 world, thousands of lives were lost and thousands more were ruined. I can't help but think of the families that were left behind, especially the little kids who lost parents that fateful day. I still think of them from time to time and wonder how they're doing.

I was starkly reminded of all those lives lost when Nico and I visited the 9/11 Museum a few years back during our East Coast college visit trip. We travelled for two weeks from Boston down to Philly and had a total blast seeing schools like Harvard, Boston College and Columbia University. For me, the most impactful part of that trip was experiencing the 9/11 Museum and the human stories that it told.

I don't know that there's any advice I can give in this letter; I just wanted you to know our family history as it unfolded in the wake of 9/11. If anything, I'd tell you that life can change in a second and you have to take full advantage of every happy moment that you have. The lost souls of 9/11 and the loved one they left behind are testimony to that reality and we owe it to them to live full and productive lives.

Goodness only knows where the balance of our time together will take us, but take a moment to remind yourselves from time to time that none of our amazing story would have happened had it not been for 9/11. In that sense, every year in early September I ask that you reflect on how 9/11 changed us all and that you say a prayer for those who paid the ultimate price on that sunny Tuesday morning in 2001.

Love,
Fafa

LETTER XI

SCHOOLED

Dear Nico, Bella and Vali,

This is the only letter that I'll send to you in the form of a poem. Even though most poems are light-hearted or even funny, the topic of this one is neither of those things: It's about what a scam getting into college in the U.S. really is. I wrote this little ditty while witnessing the four years of torture that Nico went through as he prepared to apply for college. It would be funny if the joke wasn't on all of us.

As both a student and professor, I've had experiences from Salem State College to Harvard University, and many places in between. Given those experiences, I'd like to think that I'm qualified to comment on the total rip-off that a college education in the United States has become. I say this because it isn't about educating kids anymore; it's about marketing, branding and playing off of parents' fears.

Think about this for a minute...in order for a youngster to get into a, "good school," they need grades like Einstein, be a LeBron caliber athlete and write essays worthy of a Pulitzer Prize. If that's not enough, you need a perfect SAT/ACT score and in your spare time, do so many hours of community service that you make Mother Teresa look like a slacker.

On the other hand, once you get out of college and become an adult, life in the workplace is about second chances, mentoring programs, anger management and rehab. In other words, in the U.S., we treat our children like adults and our adults like children. And that's not just wrong, it's shameful.

Unfortunately, none of this is going to change by the time any of you get out of college, so you need to learn how to work the system. The best way to do that is to prepare for college by developing your own Personal Brand. In the end, it comes down to the marketing principle known as, "Product Differentiation," which is finding ways to set yourself apart from the competition.

Remember, you have to have a unique story to tell and be able to differentiate yourself from the thousands of Straight-A, violin virtuosos that you're competing against. And let's not forget the other legions of international students that will take your spot just because they'll pay more, and in cash. The system is rigged, guys, and it's not in your favor. The only way to game it is by being different.

Nico did an exceptional job with his Personal Brand, Bella's is shaping up nicely and Vali is showing great signs of promise, too. But let's not forget what's really important: In the midst of this cynical rip-off you need to get a legitimate education. It can be done…you just have to buckle down and force an education on yourselves. Do that, and you'll be the gamer as opposed to the gamee.

SCHOOLED

At the end of every summer, an American ritual begins anew.
When we send our kids off to high school
And make them bite off more than they can chew.

It's the torture of getting into college
To which I disdainfully refer.
A shameful exercise in pressure
That no child should have to endure.

So, here's a list of admission requirements
To help those teens in the breach.
My intent is to share some realities
That your instructors aren't likely to teach.

Just know from the very beginning
That there is much you'll need to get done.

Forget about prom and pep rallies
None of this is gonna be fun.

Let's start with the very basics…
Straight A's that date back to grade six.
Break that streak and you may still have hope
If only among the lower-ranked picks.

Great grades are just the beginning
The SAT and ACT loom on the horizon.
Ace both of those and you'll be on the right path
A sure sign that your stock is 'a risin'.

Sadly for you, top scores aren't enough
On the field of sport you must also excel.
Something along the lines of Serena or LeBron,
First-namers that surely ring a bell.

Athletic prowess is a great box to check
And your exploits the fans will herald.
But you won't feel any love, because after the big game
You'll pen an essay better than F. Scott Fitzgerald.

Once that's done, don't think for a minute
That you'll steal away for a slice and a cola.
If it's Harvard you want, then your community service
Must be nothing less than a cure for Ebola.

In the spirit of balance, we must get creative
And exploit the right side of the brain.
Just when you think the worst is over
You'll be introduced to a whole new level of pain.

For what would the day be without three hours of piano
And perhaps a Carnegie Hall voice recital?

Don't be fooled, having "Opera Singer" on your resume
Isn't just nice, it's really quite vital.

The list goes on, but we'll stop here
By now, you can see where this is going.
If you can't rival Einstein by the age of sixteen
It's your entire future that you will be blowing.

The reality is that while college is important
There are many roads to achieving, "success".
The fact you can't meet these absurd expectations
Doesn't mean you'll be a permanent mess.

What is most important is that you find a way
To define happiness as you see fit.
Choose a clear path based on hard-to-achieve goals
And whatever you do, don't ever, ever quit.

In spite of what the adults proclaim
You don't have to be ranked first in the nation.
Just believe in yourself and work your butt off
Turning your life into a quest for "self-actualization".

Now, that just means be the best that you can be
At whatever it is you choose to do.
When you achieve one goal, be sure to set another
That way, your journey will never be through.

The search for your better self is really what matters
By any other advice do not be fooled.
Commit yourself now to live by these words
And in the end, trust me, you'll have been properly schooled.

LETTER XII

TEDDY

Dear Nico, Bella and Vali,

After the first few letters I wrote you guys, I started to worry that I'd run out of important stuff to talk about. I have to tell you that over the last few months as I considered subjects to cover, I never once envisioned that I'd be penning a letter about our loss of Teddy.

Since his passing on Tuesday, March 20th, 2018, I've thought a lot about, "The Turd," what he meant to each of you individually, how he impacted the family and finally, what he meant to me. Given the crazy ride we took with that little white fur-ball, I think it's important to share my most sincere feelings on what is a very sad subject.

I know that each of you loved Teddy and we all feel horrible about him leaving us. As a parent, I can say that the worst feeling is to see your kids suffering while knowing deep down that there's nothing you can do about it. I'm sad to see Teddy go, but I'm equally upset by seeing what you're going through. I'm genuinely sorry he had to leave us the way he did.

I can also say that although Teddy could be unbelievably annoying, I genuinely cared about him. As I often observed, "Teddy was an idiot, but he was OUR idiot." Ted and I actually had a lot of "alone time" together and I really enjoyed his company (especially when he wasn't peeing on the rug or chasing old ladies up a tree). We all have our favorite, "Teddy stories," so here are two of mine.

The first was the day that Santa dropped him off at the house. I'll never forget the look of joy on Vali's face when she opened the box and saw, "The Ted" for the very first time. Genuine happiness is so hard to come by and the look of pure bliss on Vali's face is an image I'll forever have in my Mind's Eye. As sad as it is to see him go, that moment was so very special, and I owe him for that.

The other favorite memory you already know about…the famous case of the 4th of July dislocated shoulder. As you'll recall, you guys were in Colombia, no one else was around and I decided to have a bonding day with The Ted. What I remember most is the look on Teddy's face when he realized we'd be hanging out by the pool together and how happy he was to be, "One of the boys."

Of course, one too many margaritas lead to some horsing around and Teddy's shoulder popped out of the socket, but we got it back in and the festivities continued. As silly as it might sound, that was one of the most fun 4th of July's I've ever had. I felt a real sense of Male Bonding with him and as we celebrate the 4th in the future, I'll be sure to send a nod his way and toast his spirit.

On a more human level, Teddy's passing has forced me to think about, and confront three very important subjects…each of which can easily be applied to our relationships with one another.

First, never say things to the people you care about that you really don't mean, because you might not get a chance to take it back. I talked some smack about The Turd and now that he's gone, I realize just how much I cared about him. For all of my comments and bad behavior, I wish he was still here. I'm going to try my hardest to apply this rule to my relationships with each of you. I hope you do the same.

Second, I was reminded of how one phone call can change your life forever. One minute I was at work and the next, I'm hurrying home to deal with our loss of Teddy. It's not like it hadn't happened to me before…I remember the call about my dad's cancer and the one that revealed my mom's dementia. Teddy's death was just another reminder that we don't know when our lives will forever be altered.

Finally, Teddy reminded me that we all have a fixed amount of time together and that nobody knows when the clock will run out. Even though we make each other mad (much like Teddy did), deep down we love each other and we should maximize the good times. If there's one thing we can all learn from this tragedy it is this…find time for the one's you love and make sure that they know you love them.

In closing, I miss The Ted. But moving forward, I'll forget about his shenanigans and trashing the house, and be sure to focus on the fun we had with him. Tossing him in the pool, getting him crazy and seeing him run around the house a million miles an hour, feeding him steak and chicken from the grill… all of it. If you do the same, you'll never forget, "Theodore" and the memory of him will be a joyful one.

With much love,
Fafa

LETTER XIII

AS THE FOURTH QUARTER BEGINS AND OVERTIME LOOMS

Dear Nico, Bella and Vali,

The below is something I wrote a few weeks back and published on the Internet. I got some really emotional responses from people I don't even know, but I think it's much more important to share the lessons I've learned with my kids. It's in the form of a football analogy, but its message is about not wasting what precious time you have on this planet. It's also about how very important it is for you to, "stay in the fight," never letting life's ups and down get the best of you. As long as you have goals and are struggling to achieve them, you'll always have a purpose, and you'll never grow old.

While I have very few regrets, I sometimes wonder how things would have turned out had I been more mature as a young man, remained consistent in my professional pursuits, and creating more of a balance between having a good time and working hard. My advice to you is to create that work/fun balance now, develop good habits and you can achieve all of your goals!!! Here we go…

…For some time now, I've likened the stages of my career to a four quarter football game. I arrived at this thinking because the life choices I made forced me to be a come-from-behind player, always believing that I could make up for lost ground and wasted time in the final minutes of every match. Now that the fourth quarter of my career has begun, I have some reflections that I'd like to share:

- I was immature and a bit of a wild man in high school, so I had to begin my university studies at State College and catch up from there.
- During my twenties, I enjoyed good success at work, but my priorities

- revolved around doing the things that young, single men are inclined to do. While a total blast, I didn't start to take my career a little more seriously until age thirty, when I became an ex-patriot in Bogota, Colombia.
- Always late for the game, the next step in the maturation process came when I got married just a few months shy of my thirty-third birthday. It was at that point I realized that life was no longer an individual competition, but a team sport.
- It was only at the age of thirty six, upon the birth of my first child, that I really put forth a genuine effort. I have three children now (19, 16 and 12) whose futures very much depend on how things go in the fourth quarter. Given their young ages and the time remaining on the clock, it's likely that this game will go into overtime.

So, to continue our American custom of turning every life challenge into a sports metaphor, here's how things are looking for me as the fourth quarter begins and overtime looms:

- Overall, I played well in the first half, but in my heart-of-hearts, I know I was inconsistent.
- The third quarter was OK, but I let too much time run off the clock before scoring again.
- As I take the field for the final stanza, I'm haunted by the self-inflicted fumbles and interceptions that put me in this come-from-behind position.
- I try to counter that negativity by reminding myself of the spectacular, life-changing plays that got me to where I am today.
- The clock is running and there are no time-outs left to be taken.
- I have to play both sides of the ball and go whistle-to-whistle on every down.
- I'm a little banged up and worried that fatigue will be a factor late in the game.

And in spite of the odds and what's at stake, I look inside myself and know that I wouldn't have it any other way. I fully acknowledge my shortcomings, and while burdened by doubt and uncertainty, I STILL WANT THE BALL. Win or lose, the outcome of this game will be decided by the tenacity of my own play. There will be no bootlegs, reverses or trick plays here, just up-the-gut football. No need for a West Coast Offense either, just Massachusetts grit and a refusal to quit. I'll run behind the blocks that my family, friends and teammates throw, thanking them as the ball advances up the field. In the spirit of smash-mouth football, there will be no mercy, no quarter, with none asked for and none given.

With the game afoot and the outcome uncertain, the only thing I know for sure is that I'll ball-out until the last play is blown dead. If it takes overtime to get the job done, so be it. And while I'm confident in my abilities, should things not go my way, I'll live with the peace of knowing that I left every strand of my being on the field of play, never once yielding to failure, disappointment or folly.

Love,
Dad

LETTER XIV

LOS ABUELITOS

Dear Nico, Bella and Vali,

Since you were babies I have encouraged each of you to embrace your Latino heritage. You truly are products of, "The Age of Globalization" and I believe it essential that your personal identities be tied closely to mom's side of the family. I have believed that since Day One and given the blatant racism spewing from the White House in recent years, I think it even more important now.

When I look back on your childhood and contemplate the Hispanic bonds that have been created for you, I keep coming back to one common denominator: Your grandparents. Mom has done an outstanding job of, "Latinizing" you guys, but without the presence, commitment and generosity of, "Los Abuelitos," you wouldn't be nearly as connected to your roots as you are today.

As the, "Gringo" in the family, I feel an eternal debt of gratitude to your grandparents for everything they've done for you. Without them, I fear that the links you have to your Colombian bloodlines would be much more limited. While I will never be able to repay the debt, I do want you to know how I feel about them and the immense respect I have for them both. I hope this letter affirms those feelings.

I'll start by saying that you should be thankful that you even have grandparents. As the youngest in my family by quite a few years, I have no recollection of my paternal grandmother and a scant memory of my grandfather (and it wasn't favorable). On my mom's side, my grandma died of cancer when I was eleven. My grandfather lasted until I was sixteen, but he wasn't exactly Mr. Personality, either.

Unfortunately, in the case of my parents, both were gone before you could really enjoy them. Grampa Dick passed away from cancer in 2007, so Vali has no memory of him. You all remember Nana Mary, but the last four years we had with her here in California were a steady descent into the darkness of dementia. They were such special people that I will always lament you're not knowing them better.

Whereas you lost out with my parents, you have been truly blessed with abuelita Nora and abuelito Humberto. Although no one can replace my own parents, when I look back over the twenty five years that I've known your abuelos I am just amazed at who they are as individuals, and as a couple. In this letter, I'll begin with a few thoughts on la abuelita and then move on to don Humberto.

At less than five feet tall, what la abuelita lacks in height, she more than makes up for in personality and spunk. Married and with her first child by nineteen (that being mom, of course), she has been the classic matriarch of the family from the get-go. Without a doubt, the old saying, "Behind every great man stands a greater woman" was written with her in mind.

I wasn't there to see it, but I can only imagine what it was like for her as a young mom to pack up and move to the U.S. when your grandpa won scholarships to study at Stanford and then at Harvard. With no English, she was not only able to navigate those waters, but she did it again in the nineteen eighties when Humberto was assigned to work at the Colombian Embassy in Washington D.C.

In terms of my own relationship with Nora, I have nothing but fond memories and total respect. That's not to say that she hasn't straightened me out on occasion when she saw something she didn't like. She definitely has, and will likely continue to do so. I know that she's just looking out for her daughter's best interests and I am totally down with that kind of loyalty.

In the early days of being married, one of my fondest memories with Nora was when mom went to study at Harvard for three months, and Nora came from Bogota to stay with Nico and me in Miami. Nico was still a toddler, so

Nora and I worked together to run the household. I still kid around with her about our days as, "roommates," but I have to say that I really enjoyed that brief time together.

Over the years, I've learned a lot from la abuelita. One thing I learned from her is to never be wasteful. Like most gringos, I was the worst when it came to serving too much food and then throwing everything out afterwards. I used to laugh at Nora when she froze half-bananas and tiny pieces of cheese, but after seeing so much hunger and privation in Latin America, she has taught me better.

She's also taught me about the importance of taking care of our money. Her line about, "La ruina empieza en la dispensa" has always stayed with me and while I'm still pretty free-wheeling with a buck, I do pay a lot more attention to, "cuidando la plata." Coming from a woman that isn't exactly broke, that's a valuable lesson that Nora taught me.

Humberto will be the first to admit that Nora's skill with a peso is a big part of the reason why they've been able to do so well financially and build their healthy collection of condos and real estate holdings. In spite of not going to university, she's just God-given smart, has a good eye for value and can size people up quickly. Those are skills that all three of you should emulate!!!

More than anything, Nora has displayed a natural ability to manage relationships with a level head and total class. Every family has its challenges (especially when the kids get married) and I marvel at how she calmly handles every type of situation. As you know, I'm not exactly Mr. Tactful and in spite of not always applying her wisdom, she stands as a great example for how to get along with people.

Moving on to your abuelito Humberto, we all know what a special man he is. Honestly, after thirty years in global trade and having been around some really smart people, I've never met anyone with the same combination of brains and willingness to work REALLY hard, as him. I've done projects with Humberto and in spite of being much younger, he worked me into the ground every time! The story I like to tell most about abuelito is how he won the, "Smartest Guy in Colombia Contest" (my words) and was awarded full-ride scholarships to Stanford for his Masters and Harvard for a PhD in Education. From there he has gone on to be a distinguished professor, highly-sought after consultant, Presidential adviser and speechwriter, and the author of dozens of books. He really is a genius.

I could go on and on about abuelito's many accomplishments, but to truly appreciate him, I think you have to look beyond the obvious. For me, he's not just brilliant, he is the ultimate expression of the main theme of almost all of my letters to you…self-actualization. Consistent with the meaning of self-actualization, I've not seen anyone take so many God-given gifts and make the absolute most of them.

It's hard to say what's motivated your grandfather to achieve such great heights. Without speaking for him, I can't help but think that some of his boundless energy comes from being diagnosed with diabetes at the age of twenty five. Such a life-changing event may have reminded him that our stay here on earth is but brief and that we have to make the most of whatever time we have.

One thing I do know is that Humberto has had a profound effect on my own journey towards self-actualization. Although I've always believed in its power, there was a period of time after Graduate School when I though I knew everything. Your grandpa called me out on my ignorance and from there, I re-committed fully to WORKING at making the most of my meager talents. I owe him for that, big time.

Another thing to know about abuelito is what I call his, "Quite Generosity." We're only aware of a few of the stories, but there are many people whose lives he's changed that we'll never hear about. From the young girl he and Nora took in off the streets, to the janitor's son at Los Andes University that he put through college, his willingness to give back to a country that's given so much to him is truly admirable.

As a couple, there is so much to admire about Humberto and Nora. They are so generous to everyone around them, but especially the immediate family. You've been on the trips paid for by them…the entire family invited on cruises, to Disney and mad Alaskan adventures. Not to mention the individual trips that you guys went on to Africa, Europe and Latin America. What great memories they've given each of you.

If it weren't for them, you wouldn't have spent your childhood summers in Colombia. It is my hope that those trips will have a permanent impact on each of you and how you identify as Latinos. Cherish those memories, build upon them and seek to create more. Los abuelos have had a profound influence on the formation of my, "American" babies and I know you wouldn't be who you are today without them.

The last advice I'll give you on the theme of your grandparents is to look at the relationship they have with mom. What they share reminds me a lot of what I had with my parents…talking to each other every day, visiting whenever possible and just taking advantage of the precious time they have together. To see them together is precisely why I always encourage mom to go to Colombia whenever she wants.

In the U.S., I know that it's pretty rare for children to have a really close relationship with their parents, especially as kids grow older. I would urge you to ignore that aspect of gringo culture and really invest in the bonds we can create together. I very much want that with you guys and I know mom does, too. Use what you see between mom and los abuelos to build the best of what a family relationship can be.

Without a doubt, we all owe a great deal to Humberto and Nora. I feel especially indebted to them for all that they've done for our family and will forever hold them in the highest regard. As a future grandad (hopefully), I can only aspire to do for your kids what they've done for mine.

Love,
Fafa

LETTER XV

GRAMPA DICK

Dear Nico, Bella and Vali,

Unlike previous letters that have dealt with life's, "Big Themes," this one is about my dad. As I've told you before, there are things that I'll never know about my father and I want to spare you the same wonderings that I've had. Oddly enough, one of the ways I hope to share more about myself is by telling you what I do know about my dad. I hope that you see a lot of him in me.

Your Grampa Dick was born Richard Henry Gardner on July 31, 1925 in Lynn, MA. Raised on 14 Atkinson Street in West Lynn, he was the oldest of six kids and was brother to his twin siblings Art and Margaret (Sis), my uncle Phil, and aunts Jean and Kathy. As of the writing of this letter, Grampa Dick is survived only by his sister, Jean.

The lack of detail about my dad's past started from childhood and continued until when he was seventeen. With that said, there are some inferences that can be made about his past based on important stories he did share with me, as well as the time frame in which they took place. It's likely that the things I don't know about him are those that most shaped his life.

For example, and by virtue of the fact that Grampa Dick was born in 1925, I know that he lived through the Great Depression and that things weren't so good. His dad was a factory guy making short money and as the oldest child, he told me that he shined shoes in McDonough Square when he was seven and that he had to stand in line for government cheese.

One pivotal moment he did tell me about was when his mom came down with tuberculosis and she got put in a sanitarium. I'm not sure of his age, but I do know that he and his five siblings were split up and sent to live with different relatives. I have no idea who he lived with or for how long, but one can only imagine the separation and vulnerability that he undoubtedly felt.

Another thing I can share is that Grampa Dick's dad, Richard Henry Maxwell Gardner wasn't a very nice guy. As the youngest in my family, I only have two recollections of him and both times he was drunk. One was of him falling out of a cab out in front of our house on Bulfinch Terrace. The other was of him sitting in a booth, stewed, at the old West Lynn bar, Frank's Sea Grill.

The first of two other stories my dad told me about his father was that upon being introduced to my mom for the first time, he farted. The other involved Grampa Dick as a young boy finding his dad having sex with a neighbor and then innocently telling his mom. That act provoked "Old Harry" to give my dad a beat down. Clearly, your great grandad was a real gem.

It's important to mention your great grandfather a bit more because the circumstances around his birth impact your lineage as true, "Americans." My dad always said that, "His people" were from the province of Newfoundland in Canada, but I wasn't so sure about that. That is, until I stumbled upon some old family documents after Grampa Dick's passing in 2007.

In my possession to this day, I found a birth certificate issued in 1972 by the province of Newfoundland & Labrador in Canada, stating that my paternal grandfather was born on June 13th, 1903 in the town of Foster's Point. That would be all we needed to prove our Canadian heritage, except I found other documents that said something different.

The first was my father's own birth certificate that states his dad was born in Philadelphia. Then, there's my father's death certificate claiming my grandfather's birthplace was Ireland. And finally, there's another birth certificate for him putting his place of birth as Lynn, MA. For all that dubiousness, I'm quite sure that my grandfather was born in Newfoundland.

Of course, the above makes each of you part Canadian, thus legitimizing you as, "True Americans." In fact, and as stated in one of my first letters, you're more American than most anyone born in the United States. Why? Because your bloodlines can be traced to both North and South America…Canada, the U.S. and Colombia. Show me another, "American" with that pedigree!!!

What really amuses me about my grandfather is that there's a possibility we are descendants of an illegal alien!!! With all the news about building walls and, "Taking our country back," I find it hilarious that my beautiful and bi-racial, "American Babies" are of even more sketchy origins.

One of the last things I'll say about my grandad is that when WWII began, he joined the Navy and left his family behind. It might be that abandonment, along with other traumatic childhood experiences that hardened my dad's emotions. I'm not sure, but such events may explain why I never once saw him cry, ever. My guess is that by the time he grew up, he was all cried out.

There are fewer gaps in Grampa Dick's story after he turned seventeen because that's when he joined the Navy. I have the full record of his time in the U.S. Navy, so I know that he enlisted on February 17, 1943, some five months short of his eighteen birthday. I also know he did boot camp at the Great Lakes and was stationed in Alameda, California and Pearl Harbor.

Grampa Dick never saw action in WWII, but he volunteered well shy of his eighteenth birthday, was available for any assignment and was honorably discharged on January 28, 1948 at Lido Beach in Long Island, NY. Based on his Navy papers, I'm happy to report that the stories he told me about his days as a sailor were consistent with his official assignments.

Your Grampa Dick was a proud member of what someone dubbed, "The Greatest Generation," which were the men and women of WWII that came home after the war, founds jobs and started families. After the war, my father studied the, "Construction Course" at Wentworth institute in Boston on the G.I. Bill, which was a government deal that offered free college to veterans.

I know that your Grampa Dick met Nana Mary at Fishermen's Beach in Swampscott, MA, through an introduction from my dad's best friend since birth, Mr. Frankie Lowry. They were married on March 25, 1951 and quickly had my sister, Kate and brother Dicky. They moved to 23 Bulfinch Terrace in Lynn, MA in 1956 to a home that was remodeled entirely by my dad.

After Wentworth, he got a job at the United Shoe Machinery Corporation up in Beverly, MA, working there for thirty eight years. Some of my fondest memories as a tike were when he'd take me with him to, "The Shoe" on Saturday mornings and then to McDonald's afterwards. Even now, I can't look at a bag of McDonald's fries without thinking of him.

My father was the classic, "provider," putting a roof over our heads, clothes on our backs and food in our bellies. We were straight up middle class and NEVER lacked for any material needs. Honestly, I can't remember a day that he ever missed work, even after coming down with tuberculosis himself and dragging his butt to The Shoe every day for the two years he was sick.

My relationship with Grampa Dick really blossomed when I was sixteen, mainly because I came of working age. He was all about the Work Ethic and when it came to his kids being gainfully employed, his motto was a simple one: "If I'm up, you're up." That meant that under no circumstances would his kids be lying in bed while he trudged off to work.

Surely you'll recall some other work-related letters about my time with Grampa Dick, like the ones about not being a, "Hammer Mechanic" or the, "Dumb End of the Tape," so I won't bore you with many more here. I will tell you that I learned a lot about respect for the Working Man through the endless jobs he got me as a construction hand, factory worker and janitor.

Looking back on the "Work Years," I cherish silly stuff, like him giving me a ride every day back and forth to a summer construction job. We'd always make two stops on the way home for a cocktail, one at The Ferry Way in Beverly and the other at the Buchanan Café in Lynn. One of my proudest moments was the first time I bought him a drink from my pay envelope.

If you ever wonder why I'm the way I am about work and my rants about, "Standing on your own two feet," "Earning your keep" or "Making your own way in this world," it's because of what my dad taught me not with words, but by his actions. Here are a few of the big lessons that have remained with me:

1. Take personal pride in the quality of any work you do
2. Be reliable
3. Keep your word, no matter what
4. Don't be a liar or a cheat
5. Always pay your debts
6. Never welch on a bet
7. Always show respect for the working man

My dad was a simple man who aspired to raising a family and doing right by his kids. My sister, brother and I were all afforded opportunities, but because I was the youngest by ten and seven years, respectively, I had more. I've always prided myself on listening to my parents' advice and taking advantage of all the things they taught, and did for me.

Ultimately, the greatest lesson he taught me now serves as my personal job description…"To leave the next generation poised for greater things." There isn't much I truly care about, but working with mom to help you achieve your dreams is at the top of the list. Be assured that I got that straight from your Grampa Dick.

In summary, here's a Short List of what he did for me:

1. Got me numerous jobs in construction, manufacturing and janitorial all over the North Shore
2. Paid for me to be an Exchange Student in Popayán, Cauca, Colombia the summer of 1980
3. Put me through college, even after transferring to the more expensive AIC
4. Got me a job as a Resident Assistant my senior year at AIC through State Rep Walter Boverini
5. Set me up with a work contact of his when I moved to Puerto Rico in the fall of 1984
6. Put his house up as collateral for a loan he got me for graduate school in 1988 (paid in full)

7. Helped "facilitate" the background check portion of my Customs Brokers license approval through Congressman Nick Mavroules (a few dubious arrests for bar fighting…it's a long story)

Your Grampa Dick wasn't all work and we had a lot of fun together. His favorite thing was being out on the ocean and we had a number of small boats from the time I was a little guy. I can remember the look of joy on his face from being on the high seas, captaining his own ship. The best were the times we went scuba diving for lobsters off the boat that he and my brother bought in 1984, the infamous, 'Qua Na'.

Some of the most fun I had with him came when I became an adult and was able to pay him back a bit for the all the good he'd done for me. Going on vacation to Northern California in 1995 with him, Nana Mary and mom was certainly a high point. So were all the winters we'd see each other in Florida when they were in Naples, and mom and I were living in Miami.

Our saddest moment came in 2005 when we were living in Guadalajara. That was the day I got the call that my dad had been diagnosed with esophageal cancer and was in the hospital. I remember vividly that it was a Sunday because mom, Nico, Bella and myself had just returned from a weekend in San Miguel de Allende. I was back in Boston the very next day.

Grampa Dick put up one heck of a fight and he lasted two years before the cancer finally got him on January 1, 2007. Honestly, I never witnessed a more dignified battle in my life. Just like I never saw my dad cry, I never once heard him complain, bitch or moan about what he was going through. I can only hope to show the same dignity should I find myself in similar circumstances.

I was there for the last weeks of his time with us and they were truly special. He wanted to die at home, so the waning days of his struggle were spent at the place that made him happiest, the house he'd bought with Nana Mary back in 1956. There were two things that happened in the final week of his life that meant the most to my relationship with him.

When someone is ready to pass away at home, it's customary to have a Hospice Caregiver involved to make sure that a patient is comfortable and safe. We had one for Grampa Dick and a few days before he died a woman came to give him a sponge bath and change his bed. Even though he only weighed about eighty pounds by then, she needed help moving him.

I consider it the single greatest privilege of my life to be able to lift my dad out of the bed he was in and carry him to the other bedroom. It lasted all of ten seconds, but the feeling of lifting him from the bed and knowing that he was literally in my hands is something I had never experienced before, or since. I can feel his meager weight and sense of total reliance right now.

In spite of the sadness that Grampa Dick's passing brought, I am eternally grateful to have had the opportunity to say goodbye to him. Lots of people experience loss without the closure of a goodbye and I'm blessed for having been able to do so. Eleven years after his death, you can be sure that I'm in tears as I share this with you.

On a late December morning in 2006 I sat next to his bed at mattress height, held his hand in both of mine and thanked him for all he'd done. I also did something we rarely did in the Gardner family; I told him that I loved him. Finally, I shared with him that in spite of all my travels and business success, I really only aspired to be like him and do right by my babies.

He couldn't say much, but I know he heard and understood me. He responded simply by saying "You're a good man" and "I'm proud of you." For all the accolades, awards and degrees I've received over the years, there is none more valuable than the approval of my father. I'm not sure how good of a man I turned out to be, but I'm certainly proud to have been his son.

I remain saddened to report that your Grampa Dick died at home at 10:00 a.m. on New Year's Day, 2007. He was surrounded by the people who cared about him most; his adoring wife Mary, daughter Kate and sons Richard Jr. and me. His funeral was held two days later in the same church where he got married, St. Pius V. I made sure that the American flag covered his coffin.

There's so much more I'd like to tell you about your Grampa Dick, but you'd be reading for hours on end. Hopefully, the details that I've provided here will be combined with the endless stories I've told you about him, and my own upbringing in Lynn. Ultimately, I want you to know that whatever good there is in me, much of it came from him and the example he set.

Love,
Dad

LETTER XVI

NANA MARY

Dear Nico, Bella and Vali,

For reasons you'll soon read, this is a very difficult letter for me to write. The relationship I had with my mom was a central theme of my life from the day I was born until her passing on May 24, 2016. Your Nana Mary was the best friend I ever had and I can't imagine how I would have turned out without her love and support. This letter is meant to explain to you just how special she really was.

Your paternal grandmother, Mary Ellen McDonald Gardner, was born on August 12, 1929 in Lynn, Massachusetts. She was the middle child between her older brother Joe (deceased) and her younger sister, Ruthie. Her childhood seemed relatively uneventful and like most young ladies of her generation she graduated high school (1947), met a WWII veteran, got married and raised a family.

As is the case in most unique relationships, ours was born of circumstance, timing and personalities. Because my brother and sister were seven and ten years older than me, and they both moved out at the age of eighteen, I was more or less an only child from the age of eleven on. That gave my mom and me a big head start towards building what became a profound friendship.

The fact that Grampa Dick worked a lot and spent a fair amount of his free time at haunts like the Buchanan Café, meant that Nana Mary and I had even more alone time. From the earliest days, I can recall baking cakes and cookies with her, going shopping at department stores like Filene's Basement in Boston, Hoffman's in downtown Lynn, or having a slice of pizza at Caruso's on Union St.

When I think about the time I spent with my mom and all the things we did together, I just don't understand why some kids today go through a, "phase" in which they're embarrassed to be seen with their parents, or don't want to be around them at all. Assuming a parent cares about their kids in the first place, I find such an attitude to be a waste of life and something that never occurred to me, ever.

For example, my high school (Lynn English) happened to be just a mile away from the elementary school where my mom worked as a Teacher's Aide. Every morning for three years, Nana Mary took me to school in her blue Nova and dropped me off in plain sight, for all the world to see. I have no recollection of ever being embarrassed or feeling like a pansy because my mom drove me.

As an adult, we went clothes shopping together quite a bit, too. Perhaps it was a carryover from childhood, but right up until I moved away at age thirty, Nana Mary came shopping with me and helped pick out my stuff. I'll always remember her saying in that Boston accent, "You can neva' go wrong with a blue blaza' and a nice pair of chinos." Even now, I can't walk into a Marshall's without thinking of her.

The reality is that there are plenty of kids that don't have a parent in their lives and even if they do, many of them aren't up to the task of loving a child. I saw plenty of that growing up and I always had a sense of being really lucky to know that my parents loved me. They certainly weren't perfect, but I believed that they had my best interests in mind and I had no intention of squandering my good fortune.

As you have seen, mom and I aren't perfect either, but we love each of you and are committed to helping you make your way in this life. No two relationships are alike, but if we can come close to what I had with my parents and what mom has with hers, I'll consider myself a success. Let's not waste whatever time we have together on silly bickering or stuff that in the end, really isn't important.

Changing gears a bit, the first really important conversation I had with Nana Mary was when I was fourteen years old. I had done the math on the years that separated me and my siblings, and having learned about the Birds & the Bees, I asked her if my birth was an accident. I still have the mental picture of my mom standing at the ironing table next to our kitchen table as she answered.

I don't know if she had anticipated my question in advance, but the sweetness with which she told the story made me feel loved. First, she told me that she had two miscarriages after my brother was born and that the doctor said she couldn't have any more children. I suspect my dad took that news as an invitation to be less cautious in his marital activities and as it turned out, all the better for me.

Then, her exact words were, "You weren't an accident, you were a pleasant surprise." It's no coincidence I have such a vivid recollection of that scene, because I soon decided that given the circumstances, I was on some cosmically ordained "Bonus Plan." I think that conversation had much to do with the wanderlust and sense of adventure I developed a few years later.

We shared a deep love for each other, but Nana Mary wasn't always rainbows and unicorns. She was tough as nails and didn't hesitate to hand out a verbal dress-down or a physical assault if she deemed one necessary. In that vein, it's only fitting that she had beautiful, fiery red hair and was known by all as, "Big Red." For the record, the few times that she cuffed me around, it was well deserved.

The best story about Nana Mary's temper was when I was a freshman at Salem State and living at home. That was the year prior to leaving for AIC, but I was already acting like I was out on my own. There were a couple of weekends when I came home way past curfew and one time, I didn't come home at all. Nana Mary was having none of that, and the final straw came when she laid the perfect trap for me.

The next time I was late, Mary had the house on lockdown. I usually had a few ways to sneak in, but without any keys, I had no option but to ring the bell. She let me in and once the door was closed, she KO'd me with a single shot to the jaw. When I came to, she was gone and my dad was standing over me in his boxer shorts and white T-shirt. All's he said was, "You're an asshole" and marched off to bed.

I don't remember what time I woke up the next morning, but Nana Mary was waiting for me in the kitchen where she had told me five years earlier that I was no accident. She started in on me with one of her more famous lines, "You don't know how to act!" and then informed me that I'd have to move away to finish college. When my parents dropped me off at AIC nine months later, she cried like a baby.

In stark contrast to her (mildly) aggressive side, Nana Mary was a devout Catholic. I didn't realize it until later in life, but within the Catholic Church she was known as a, "Marian," or someone who is devoted to the Virgin Mary. Given her name, I probably should have figured that out sooner, especially since whenever she spoke of being Catholic, it was always about, "The Blessed Mutha."

I'm sure Nana Mary was disappointed that her three kids dropped Catholicism. In my case, it came in 7th grade when I not only switched from St. Pius to Pickering Junior High, but also when I got caught skipping church. Since I was her third pagan child she was probably tired of talking about it by the time I got caught. From that day forward, she never mentioned going to church again and I didn't go back.

When I got a little older and really began to question religion, I used to rib her about giving cash to St. Pius every week, and how she was a sap for doing so. Then, when my dad got cancer and I thought she would surely lose her mind, Nana Mary found peace in her faith. I saw the strength and solace that her beliefs gave her, and that was fine by me. After all, isn't that what religion is supposed to do?

Just so you know, I'm not disappointed that you guys aren't into organized religion. I do hope that you believe in some sort of Creator and that you communicate with him/her in your own personal way. I have no answers on faith and neither does anyone else. What I do know is that Nana Mary found peace in her religion and that's what matters. May you do the same with whatever yours turns out to be.

With our minor religious differences aside, I think part of the reason why Nana Mary and I got along so well was that I listened to both her and my father. Like I said before, I always believed they had my best interests in mind and I trusted their judgment. After all, it was Mary that first got me into Spanish and put me into typing class in high school. Clearly, those two moves helped me out big time.

When I got to college and on to graduate school, our relationship changed from one of advice to guidance and support. Neither of my parents had gone to college (Grampa Dick went to trade school), so when I had to make decisions about my major, classes to take etc., they trusted in my judgement. Those decisions worked out well, but Nana Mary was also there when things got rough.

As noted in another letter, a few months after I graduated college, I left on an adventure to Puerto Rico that ended with me returning a month later with my tail between my legs. After a successful college career and the highest of expectations, that was a big fall, and it was Nana Mary that consoled and encouraged me afterwards. Apart from my mom and dad, I don't remember anyone else helping me up.

Nana Mary was also there when my second book, "Tortoise Riskies" turned out to be a flop. I had arranged a book signing at a Barnes & Noble in Peabody, MA and even advertised it in the Lynn newspaper. When nobody showed up for it, it was Nana Mary that stayed the whole time to keep me company. Again, I don't recall a lot of other people being there for that disaster of a day.

As each of you sets audacious goals and works to achieve them, you too will face difficulties, as well as outright failure. When you do, just know that mom and I will be there to lend a hand as you dust yourselves off and get back in the fight. Trust me, it's a lot easier to confront a failure or a bad decision when your parents have your back. We definitely have yours.

If someone were to say to me, "Choose one word that describes your relationship with your mom," it would be, "Fun." As simple as it sounds, we enjoyed each other's company and had fun together. Whether it was the holidays, an Italian meal in Boston's North End, or all the time we spent together when she and my dad wintered in Florida, we just really like being together.

Thinking back, the most fun we had wasn't at events like the holidays or a birthday. It was the regular, every day stuff like watching a few innings of a Red Sox game, talking at the kitchen table over breakfast or sitting out in the back yard in summertime. Mary was such a good listener and I felt that she was always hanging on my every word. I'm so glad I had her as my mom.

For all the things that Nana Mary did for me and all the great times we had together, in the end, I feel like I failed her. Back around 2012 when I began to hear about her showing early signs of dementia, I travelled to Lynn to see for myself. She was in a dark place, doing weird stuff like cutting up junk mail into a million pieces, and I made a spot decision to bring her out to California to live with us.

You guys were just kids, but surely Nico and Bella recall some of the episodes at the house and the fast education we all got in what dementia really is. I not only plucked Nana Mary from the only home she ever knew, but I grossly underestimated what it would take to care for her during what turned out to be a four year journey into total darkness.

I credit your mom with doing the hard work of finding the best care for Nana Mary. After we realized it was unsafe for her to be at home with us, it was mom that found every facility we put her in during that four year odyssey. As her condition worsened, mom also suggested many of the necessary changes that needed to be made to keep her safe and comfortable. I won't soon forget those acts of kindness.

Even though Nana was well looked after, I feel like I failed her because I put her care in the hands of strangers. In spite of knowing that she would have ended up in a home no matter what, I still feel guilty about it. Seeing her go through a series of falls that ended with a black eye, broken wrist and fractured hip really didn't do much to make me feel better.

There's no good way to die, but dementia is an especially cruel illness. Apart from the physical toll it takes, its greatest cruelty is that it robs a person of their self-awareness. Even worse, in the early stages of dementia, the patient knows it. In talking to my mom about her disease, she ran the gamut from speaking through tears of how scared she was, to saying laughingly, "I think I'm losing my marbles!"

After a while, I began to gauge the progression of Nana Mary's sickness by the people she stopped talking about. Early on, she told me a bunch of times that her mother had just come to visit. Esther died of cancer in 1971, so the fact that she spoke of her so sweetly told me that although she never mentioned it, she missed her mom dearly. Within a few months, those imaginary visits stopped.

A short time after that, she then stopped talking about my dad. Stripped of all emotional pretense, it was clear that she truly loved my dad and she sobbed about his passing frequently. And then, from one day to the next, there was no more talk of him, either. And so the story went until the only people she remembered from back in the day were my sister (who visited faithfully) and me.

As you know, Nana Mary's final months were at a dementia facility in Fullerton, California. Over time, dementia wears a person down physically and she ended up in a wheel chair, unable to walk. Her last lap started when she fell ill and I took her to the E.R. for a battery of tests that nearly killed her. I'll never forget the sound of her screaming in pain from a catheter the technicians just couldn't get inserted.

In spite of all the tests the E.R. doctor put Nana Mary through, when he went over the results with me it was clear he wasn't paying attention. In fact, when he showed me her chest X-rays on a computer screen, he didn't say a word until my own untrained eye pointed to a cloudiness over her left lung. That turned out to be viral pneumonia.

Nana Mary was admitted to the hospital and from there, things went south quickly. I spent a long night on a recliner in her room and the next morning the Admin people asked me about signing a document that authorized them to stop treatment. That meant that they'd keep her comfortable, but there would be no more meds for the pneumonia. Essentially, they were asking me to sign her Death Warrant.

Before I go any further, I want you to take this letter as an instruction that if something similar should happen to me, you are to sign the same authorization, without hesitation. It killed me to do it, but I knew that if I didn't it would only prolong her suffering and drag out a story to which there was no happy ending. I signed, and if you ever find yourselves in similar circumstances, you are to do the same.

Mary was discharged and returned to the home in Fullerton, where she passed away at 3 p.m. on May 24th, 2016. Just as it was with my dad, I consider myself blessed to have been at her side at the time of her passing. I had the opportunity to tell her I loved her one last time and to thank her for being my best friend. She had strength enough to say, "I love you too, sweetheart" and within an hour, she was gone.

There isn't a day that goes by that I don't think about both of my parents. Ours was a special bond and I attribute a great deal of the happiness I've found in this life to the relationship I had with them. They brought me joy when they were alive and the memories of our time together will be a source of great comfort until my own time comes.

After reading the letters about my mom and dad, it should be clear to you why my number one goal in life is to, "Leave the next generation poised for greater things." My parents lifted me up in ways they likely never realized and it's my job to do the same for you. I believe that my greatest source of joy in the future will come from the times that we all share together. I hope you feel the same way.

Love,

Fafa

LETTER XVII

THE SEEKER

Dear Nico, Bella and Vali,

From the moment I wrote my first letter to you, I had three goals in mind. First, I wanted to share my thoughts on life's "Big Themes," the biggest of which is defining happiness on your own terms. Next, I wanted to make sure that as biracial kids you know who you are and where you came from. Lastly, I felt the need to open up about myself and the life experiences that defined me.

While my objectives were clear, I had no idea the type of emotional journey those letters would take me on. Honestly, I thought it would be easy to choose important subjects to write about, jog my memory for relevant life experiences and put them down on paper. What I quickly learned was that to, "Keep it real" I'd have to look deep inside myself, going all the way back to my earliest days.

What's ironic is that although I set out to try and help you guys, my letters turned out to be unbelievably helpful to me. The process of selecting topics, exploring my innermost feelings and writing about them welled up emotions in me that spanned jubilation, sadness, satisfaction and nostalgia. Regardless of the feelings evoked by each letter, I'm glad I wrote every one of them.

Please know that this letter is not intended to signify an end to my writings. On the contrary, consider it a pause where you can reflect on what our exchanges have meant to you thus far. Personally, I've taken great joy in the, "What did you learn?" talks we've had after each letter. Now, I feel like it's time for me to share my own learnings and observations. Let's complete the circle with the story of, "The Seeker."

As I explained to Bella recently, The Seeker is actually a song by one of my all-time favorite rock bands, "The Who." Although it came out in 1971, I didn't hear it for the first time until I was a freshman at Salem State College in 1980. Since that time, and for a number of different reasons, The Seeker became a kind of personal anthem for me.

I've often told you this, but I knew I had to leave Salem State within the first few weeks of classes starting. Bearing in mind that I began there just days after returning from a summer as an Exchange Student in Colombia, I needed a lot more excitement to keep me entertained. For the record, Salem State was a great experience and as random as it sounds, their FM radio station was pretty good, too!

In what became a routine, I used to tune into the Salem State radio station every morning while I got ready for school. Back then, the student DJ's took song requests by phone and once I got turned on to The Seeker, I was constantly phoning in the request. I still remember how cool it was to call in and then a few minutes later, be rocking out to my newly adopted theme song.

Whereas this story might sound like a simple, "Blast from the Past," it's much more than that. I'm sharing it because it was also around the same time that I learned about another of my Big Themes, "Self-actualization." Tied once again to Salem State, it was in a class on Western Civilization that I was introduced to the belief that happiness can be found through living up to one's full potential.

So, if you think about it, within a one year period I had a life-altering travel experience, I discovered a philosophy that touched me to the core and I was able to put a name to the whole vibe by borrowing a title from a Who song. From that point forward, I lived my Seeker's Creed through the pursuit of self-actualization and by doing that, I was defining happiness on my own terms.

That's some pretty heavy stuff for an eighteen year-old to come up with, but as I reflect back on all of the highs, lows, successes and failures I've had across the years, I remain true to that philosophy. I believe in it as much today as I did almost forty years ago and I'll go to the grave living the Seeker's mentality of pushing the envelope, every day.

All of the thoughts and memories that my letters conjured up caused me to evaluate how my Life Philosophy has turned out. After all, no one wants to commit to a Belief System only to realize that it was misguided, or a total bust. While my life's journey has been neither of those things, I can say that a series of changing priorities did cause me to alter my definition of what a Seeker should be.

With that said, here are some of the observations, reflections and advice that my letter writing has inspired me to share with you:

1. In my early years of adulthood, I defined happiness as self-actualization through a constant search for challenges, freedom and adventure. Be it in academics, my career progression, personal relationships or how I approached life in general, I was all about the action. Basically, I got a rush from being in a hurry, and I loved every minute of it.

   The thrill I got from being an Action Junkie was the driving force of the better part of my youth. Given its importance, I've put a lot of thought into that pattern of behavior and realized that I was as much running away from boredom as I was chasing action. That might sound odd, but it's true. As a young man in my twenties, I was scared to death that every day would be identical to the one before it.

2. In spite of the, "Devil take tomorrow" sound to all this, the truth is that I was able to define happiness on my own terms by pure luck. First off, after my older brother was born and my mom had two miscarriages, she was told there'd be no more babies. Of course, I paid no attention to that diagnosis and I've been on the, "I wasn't supposed to be here anyway, so why not go for it?" plan ever since.

   Second, I was born a white male in the United States at the end of the Baby Boom. Now, I know there are a lot of people out there (mostly white males, BTW) that say, "White Boy Advantage," is a myth. As a White Boy myself who has benefitted big time from my gender and skin tone, I can tell you 100% that White Boy Advantage is real, and that it was a big part of the good fortune that was sent my way.

While the whole, "I was never supposed to be here in the first place" story might be a bit of a stretch, my real luck came from having parents that loved and supported me. From Day One, they did everything possible to, "Leave the next generation poised for greater things" and I was there to take the baton. Not every kid is afforded that blessing and I'm eternally grateful for it.

3. If there's one down side to self-actualization, it's the, "Self" part. There have been periods when my pursuit of happiness caused me to abuse important relationships, and people close to me paid the price for it. Be advised that self-actualization taken to an extreme is just another word for selfish and in the end, it does way more harm than good. Try to avoid that as you pursue your own version of happiness.

4. Luckily, I also realized early on that self-actualization doesn't always have to be about self. To the contrary, one of the greatest senses of accomplishment that one can feel is through helping others. In yet another ironic twist, I came to this realization not because of an innate desire to serve others, but out of my own selfishness. Basically, I became a teacher to offset how badly I was feeling about myself.

We all know that I've been a part-time professor of global trade for my entire adult life. What you might not know is that I came to teaching because I was out of control in my early twenties and got into some trouble with the law. I've told you parts of the story before, but the gist is that I was in a few bar fights that in addition to creating some legal problems, had me feeling like a real loser.

It was during that time I decided that instead of being a menace to society, I should do something to help improve it. Because the office of the shipping company I worked for was next to Logan Airport, I had easy access to one of the city's biggest and most diverse neighborhoods, East Boston. It was there that I got my first job teaching the GED to immigrants from Cambodia and Central America.

You can learn a lot from teaching and the exposure I had to people that survived near-death experiences humbled me. That statement is no exaggeration because my students were Cambodians that escaped the genocide of Pol Pot and my Central American students were fleeing civil wars in Nicaragua and El Salvador. A vision of their faces and their stories of death, loss and suffering are with me still.

Since that time, I've taught and lectured on four continents at universities that include my alma maters AIC and U Miami, ASU, the Tec de Monterrey in Mexico, Los Andes in Bogota and USC. After all that high flying stuff, the greatest satisfaction I ever felt from teaching came from helping those young adults get their GED's in the converted basement of a Three Decker apartment building in East Boston, MA.

As I reflect on my time as a teacher and how it helped so profoundly with my own self-actualization, I'm reminded of a quote by the economist, John Kenneth Galbraith. I've read a bunch of his books, but the most important message I got from him is that, "You can do well by doing good." Should you decide as adults to help others in their journeys, you'll come to understand the full meaning of his words.

5. Reaching your potential is about the ability to compete, but not in the way you might think. There is no denying that life is about competing. Dating back to pre-historic man, competition determined who got the cave and who ate the meat. The same tenets of competition exist today, just in a slightly more civilized format. When it comes to self-actualization, this type of competition is only part of the story.

Part of the attraction of reaching your potential is that at some point, you'll have to compete with yourself. Everyone can't be Bill Gates or Michael Jordan, so we mortals have to come to the realization that we have very human limits. That reality should never mean that we simply give in and stop competing, however, because pushing your own limits is where the real beauty of self-actualization lies.

The perfect illustration of this point is my own experience with sports. By the time I was in seventh grade, I knew I didn't have the talent to be a top athlete at anything. I loved all kinds of sports, though, and even after "retiring" from organized team events in the tenth grade, I kept competing. And that was when I embraced a more personal meaning of the verb, "to compete."

As a young guy, I still played pick-up games of basketball, but I focused on activities where I could compete against myself. Whether it was an extra lap in the pool, one more rep on the bench press or a minute longer on my bike, that was the kind of competition I enjoyed the most. There was only one person who knew if I gave my all, only one judge of the results and I came to love that feeling.

6. The last thing I'll say about being a Seeker (for now) is that as your priorities change and evolve, so should your seeking. As you can hopefully see, happiness through fulfilling your potential comes in many forms and it's OK to make adjustments along the way. For me, those changes started when I married mom and really began to come full circle when you three were born.

To be honest with you, I put more thought into this letter than any of the previous ones. Because I knew this would be the last of my writings for a while, the truth is I wanted to come up with a dramatic close that would stay with you guys forever. I literally searched my soul in the dark of the night and my thoughts finally came together. Here's how they role…

In closing, I'll say the same thing to you at the beginning of your lives that I said to my dad at the end of his. You know this from the letter entitled, "Grampa Dick," but I had a chance to say goodbye to my father a few days before his passing. It was the opportunity of a lifetime to thank him for everything he'd done for me, as well as to let him know how I felt about being his son.

I told him that after years of seeking and all of the things I'd done, I only wanted to be like him. Just like he had done for me, I assured him that my mission was to leave my beautiful American Babies poised for greater things. And like he had Nana Mary as his partner in that endeavor, I consider myself fortunate to have mom as mine. So should you.

In the final analysis, reaching our full potential is about time and how we use it to enrich not just our own lives, but those of the people around us. The funny thing about time is that it's the most precious asset any one of us has, but we don't realize how valuable it is until it's gone. And in the ultimate practical joke, God doles out time to each of us on a clock with no hands.

With you guys growing up so quickly, mom and I noticed that the five of us share less and less time as a family. In fact, when we were all reunited this past Thanksgiving, mom made the observation that with her and Vali in Colombia all last summer, and Nico returning to Vanderbilt before they got home, the Friday before Thanksgiving was the first time we had all been together in six months.

You might not recall, but right when Nico got home from Vanderbilt, we were all sitting on the couch, talking for what amounted to about fifteen minutes. After six months apart, we had a brief moment where it was just us, chatting and catching up. There was no fighting over broken curfews, lectures on mediocre grades or yapping over missing clothes. It was just us talking and boy, was that magical.

Andy Warhol, the New York artist and cultural icon from the sixties and seventies famously said that, "Everyone gets their fifteen minutes of fame." I never set out on my Grand Adventure looking for either fortune or fame, so I can say with confidence that I'd much rather have fifteen minutes with you than a lifetime in the lime light.

In the simplest of terms, self-actualization is about getting a little bit better every day at the things you deem important. Your futures are very important to me, but so is our present. To that end and with clock in hand, I'm going to seek to be a better parent, husband, friend and teacher.

Love,

Fafa